BLIND FAITH

BLIND FAITH

OUR MISPLACED TRUST IN THE STOCK MARKET —AND SMARTER, SAFER WAYS TO INVEST

by Edward Winslow

BK

BERRETT-KOEHLER PUBLISHERS, INC.
San Francisco

Berrett-Koehler Publishers, Inc.
235 Montgomery Street, Suite 650
San Francisco, CA 94104-2916
Tel: (415) 288-0260 Fax: (415) 362-2512 www.bkconnection.com

Ordering Information
Quantity sales. Special discounts are available on quantity purchases by corporations, associations, and others. For details, contact the "Special Sales Department" at the Berrett-Koehler address above.
Individual sales. Berrett-Koehler publications are available through most bookstores. They can also be ordered direct from Berrett-Koehler: Tel: (800) 929-2929; Fax: (802) 864-7626; www.bkconnection.com
Orders for college textbook/course adoption use. Please contact Berrett-Koehler: Tel: (800) 929-2929; Fax: (802) 864-7626.
Orders by U.S. trade bookstores and wholesalers. Please contact Publishers Group West, 1700 Fourth Street, Berkeley, CA 94710. Tel: (510) 528-1444; Fax: (510) 528-3444.

Berrett-Koehler and the BK logo are registered trademarks of Berrett-Koehler Publishers, Inc.

Printed in the United States of America
Berrett-Koehler books are printed on long-lasting acid-free paper. When it is available, we choose paper that has been manufactured by environmentally responsible processes. These may include using trees grown in sustainable forests, incorporating recycled paper, minimizing chlorine in bleaching, or recycling the energy produced at the paper mill.

Library of Congress Cataloging-in-Publication Data
Winslow, Edward, 1954–
    Blind faith : our misplaced trust in the stock market—and smarter, safer ways to invest : stop gambling, start investing / by Edward Winslow.
        p. cm.
    Includes bibliographical references and index.
    ISBN 1-57675-252-6
    1. Investments. 2. Portfolio management. 3. Investment analysis.
I. Title
HG4521.W4897 2003
332.6—dc21   2002038479

First Edition
08 07 06 05 04 03   10 9 8 7 6 5 4 3 2 1

Interior Design: Gopa & Ted2   Proofreader: Donna Bettencourt
Copy Editor: Judith Brown   Indexer: Medea Bogdanovich
Production: Linda Jupiter, Jupiter Productions

To Dad

Your tireless dedication to family, work, and frugality will always be an inspiration.

CONTENTS

PART III: SMARTER AND SAFER INVESTMENTS

THE JOURNEY

M Y FIRST EXPOSURE to the stock market was as a six-year-old child in 1960. My dad took me into a Merrill Lynch office near downtown Miami, Florida. I was wide-eyed and impressed with all of the activity going on in the office. There was a group of older men in the lobby area who would watch the screen and occasionally go over to the quote machine to check on a particular stock. One of the men showed me how the machine worked. I found it fascinating as he put letters in and it gave him numbers back.

The old men seemed like a generally grumpy bunch, and I came to understand that some of them spent the entire day in the office checking on their money. I remember feeling sad for them. It certainly would have been more fun to go to the beach, fish, and walk the dog, anything but be in an office all day.

The people who impressed me the most were those who called themselves stockbrokers. They were well dressed and important looking. They had a certain air about them that implied that they had lots of knowledge and intelligence. Some were constantly on the phone, making what I was sure were very important business deals.

After that first visit, I kept pestering my dad to take me back to Merrill Lynch so I could play with the quote machine. He took me a few more times, and I decided that when I grew up I wanted to be a stockbroker.

As I grew older I began to read everything I could about business and economics. I decided that a good stockbroker should be able to look at a balance sheet or income statement and evaluate whether or not a particular company was a good investment. I went to college with the intention of becoming a stockbroker. I chose to major in accounting so that I would have a strong foundation to complement the degree in business administration. During my senior year of high school I worked as an accountant for a subsidiary of United Airlines and throughout college held various accounting jobs.

But I didn't want to be an accountant. I wanted to be a stockbroker. In 1976, at the age of twenty-two, I took and passed all sections of the CPA exam on my first attempt. Although the stock market was still recovering from the huge drop of 1972 and 1973, I felt it was time to become a broker and realize my lifelong ambition. I began to interview with the large brokerage firms. After several interviews I had a sobering realization.

The interview I remember most vividly is the one that I had with Merrill Lynch. This was the firm that I was exposed to many years earlier and in my mind was the biggest, the most prestigious, and the best. Boy, was I in for a shock! In the interview I emphasized my knowledge and experience of accounting, financial analysis, and economics. The interviewer told me, "All that crap won't do you any good here. We're looking for salesmen. We tell you what to sell and train you in how to sell it. We're looking for people with a basic background in sales whom we can mold into productive stockbrokers. Brokers are salespeople, period. We have other people in the firm that analyze stuff."

I remember on my way out of the Merrill Lynch office I looked at the stockbrokers in their little cubicles and had a totally different perspective. I actually overheard a broker doing one of probably hundreds of cold calls. It went something like this: "Hello Mr. Smith. I'm Jim James with Merrill Lynch. I'm not trying to sell you anything. We have a research report on the auto industry that I'm sure you'd find valuable. I'd like to send you a copy at no charge and no obligation . . ."

Before becoming a broker with Merrill Lynch, Suze Orman, the best-selling financial author and TV personality, was a waitress for the Buttercup Bakery in Berkeley, California. Why would Merrill Lynch hire a waitress? According to Ms. Orman: "They weren't hiring a waitress. What they saw in me was that I would be an excellent saleswoman."

I decided to do some research and determine exactly how and where my training and talent could be valuable outside the accounting area. At the time, a relatively new concept was catching on called *comprehensive financial planning*. The theory was that individuals could meet with a financial planner who was educated in all aspects of individual financial decision making. This included not only investments but also tax planning, estate planning, retirement planning, and personal risk management. The planner could review an individual's financial situation and give constructive recommendations as to the best course for achieving his or her objectives.

This made a lot of sense to me, so I began to broaden my knowledge beyond the accounting and tax matters that I felt comfortable with from my experience, college degree, and study for the CPA exam. Within about three years I became a Certified Financial Planner (CFP), Chartered Life Underwriter (CLU), Chartered Financial Consultant (ChFC), Fellow in the Life Management Institute (FLMI) and an Associate in Risk Management (ARM). I also became a licensed securities broker, a life and health agent, and a property/casualty agent. There were lots of exams and lots of studying, but I felt it was all necessary to be a good financial planner.

I've been a financial advisor since 1982 and am well trained in all of the theoretical aspects of financial planning. However, I have always felt that there was something missing when it came to managing the risks of investing. There is just too much uncertainty in the world to feel with absolute confidence that stock-related investments should be the centerpiece of an individual's investment plan. I was never really at ease with this concept, and my level of discomfort increased tremendously in the late 1990s as the market soared ever higher.

My attitude relating to investments has changed dramatically since those naïve visits to a brokerage firm as a child. I've developed a personal philosophy and have come to conclusions that are at odds with traditional investment management. My hope is that this book reaches people who are questioning the whole investment process and wondering if there is a better way. I believe there definitely is!

ACKNOWLEDGMENTS

I must first give special thanks to Laura Winslow, my wife and partner. Her love, support, and critical eye made the "wild idea" of writing an investment book that could make a difference become a reality.

Thanks to the professional staff at Berrett-Koehler and the hands-on editorial direction from founder and publisher Steven Piersanti. His enthusiasm for disseminating the message of the book was extremely encouraging and his help in constructing the book invaluable.

Chris Coccaro's intimate knowledge of market-linked certificates of deposit was of tremendous value. Richard Torgerson's comments and insights relating to the area of index-linked notes was of great significance.

The reviews of the initial manuscript were very helpful. Sandy Chase, Bob Coleman, Charles Dorris, Jon Naar, and "Tip" Parker all gave significant feedback that helped narrow my focus to the most important issues. Thanks also to Mike O'Brien for his candid remarks, Barbara Taylor for her insightful comments, and Dr. Dennis Glick for his comments and assistance with investor psychology.

I was impressed with the value added during the copyediting process thanks to Judith Brown. Kudos to Linda Jupiter for putting it all together and Donna Bettencourt for her unrelenting pursuit of the missed comma.

Vicki Robin, Ed Rochette, and Alisa Gravitz early on were strong supporters of the book, and I thank them for their endorsements. I also want to thank all my clients who encouraged me to help others by getting my views down in writing.

Edward Winslow
Jacksonville, Oregon
February 2003

INTRODUCTION

BEYOND BLIND FAITH—
THERE IS CLARITY

A s A SOCIETY, we have placed our faith, hope, trust, and dreams in the upward movement of future stock prices. The wisdom of tying 50, 60, 70 percent or more of our financial net worth to this mechanism is based on the unquestioned underlying assumption that over the long run an investment in stock—a percentage share of ownership in a corporation—is the best place to put our money. As you will discover, this is a myth that we individual investors have come to blindly believe.

As investors we have experienced the jubilation of a roaring bull market and the horrible carnage wrought by a grisly bear market accompanied by colorful corporate scandals. This occurred during a time when our retirement plans accounted for about half of the country's traded stocks. Many investors feel "wiped out" by the experience and swear never to be fooled again.

Yet others, who had a solid respect for the risk of tying their savings to the market, captured much of the tremendous gains of the late 1990s and gave little or none of it back when the bottom fell out in the early 2000s. These "protected" investors recognize that at times the market is a money-generating machine and at other times a destroyer of wealth. This simple realization, that the market can move dramatically and unpredictably both up and down, calls for an investment plan that works in this perpetual high-risk environment. This book lays out that plan.

If unprotected against loss, an investment in stock or an equity mutual fund is nothing more than a gamble. Just as a fortunate few at the casino will walk away winners, while the majority of the players lose, the rules of this game favor the "house." The people at the top rake in obscene truckloads of money in frenzied rising markets and even make carloads when the market is going down.

Investors have every right to feel taken advantage of as they discover that the playing field was never level. High-profile corporate and accounting scandals provide a target for our anger and frustration as we attempt to make sense of it all.

Despite everything that has happened, financial books, magazines, and advisers stick with the same old tired line: buy and hold stocks. We need a radical diversion from this traditional investment counsel. *Blind Faith* presents an unorthodox view that will forever change your belief about the wisdom of gambling your hard-earned dollars in the stock market.

THE FOUR MAIN MESSAGES

This book has four essential messages summarized as follows:

1. The risk of placing money into common stock or equity mutual funds has evolved to the point where this process, commonly referred to as investing, can now be more accurately described as speculation or gambling.

2. The people who place money into the stock market take on most of the risk but receive only the "crumbs" of a market advance. The real winners are the executives, the corporations, and the brokerage industry. The rewards are so great that the behavior of these "beneficiaries" of market advances can range from unethical transgressions to outright fraud.

3. The traditional measures for dealing with market risk—asset allocation and diversification—do not ade-

quately address the problem. This book presents a new philosophy and strategy for dealing with the inherent dangers of stock market investing.

4. There are ways to participate in market advances while protecting the underlying principal against loss. These "protected" investment alternatives are available today and are evaluated as a means for intelligently dealing with market uncertainty.

These four messages are pertinent to anyone concerned about the risk associated with investing in stocks. This includes individuals, fiduciaries, and financial professionals, both foreign and domestic.

An underlying theme is that there is no certainty when it comes to predicting how the market will perform during a specific period of time in the future. It may turn out to be the best place to put money or the absolute worst. Investors don't know. Investment advisers don't know. Nobody knows!

Given that the future is completely uncertain, there is a better way to plan and invest that goes far beyond placing our blind faith in the expectation of an ever-rising stock market. Speculating in the market may be stimulating entertainment, but the risks associated with investing in stock are incredibly high. Investments that protect our principal yet allow for participation in the upside of the market eliminate the gambling facet and allow us more control over our future financial health.

The book is divided into three parts. Part I outlines the problem and the tremendous risk associated with stock market investing. Part II presents a logical strategy as well as a philosophy for dealing with our uncertain financial future. Part III describes specific types of investment products that can be utilized to implement the strategy, gives pointers on how to invest for retirement, and offers suggestions for improving the current capital system.

THE AVERAGE INVESTOR SHOULD
STEER CLEAR OF STOCKS—HERE'S WHY

Individuals who invest in stocks and managed mutual funds do not achieve returns that even come close to the overall market. In Part I, you will see that professionals can't beat the market either. You will also discover that certain hazards, rarely considered, create uncertainty with stock market investing. Hazards increase the risk of investing in stocks and reduce the chances of winning.

Superior intellect and a logical mind can't offset the irrational behavioral and emotional factors that go into investment decision making. The risk of investing in corporations goes far beyond normal business and economic risks because the pressures for short-term positive stock performance create a myopic view of the future. These risks became very apparent during the early 2000s as many companies imploded under dark clouds of unethical transgressions.

As investors, we have discovered that much of the research and advice distributed by the brokerage industry was totally self-serving and worse than worthless. Those who followed the advice of the large brokerage institutions during the collapse of the market bubble in early 2000 suffered big-time losses as analysts privately called the same stocks they were recommending pieces of junk.

We buy stocks and equity mutual funds with the realization that there is some risk but that the risk can be offset by higher returns. But the risks, compared to the potential rewards, are totally out of proportion. We risk losing our entire investment, while stock options grant high-paid executives a free lottery ticket to riches beyond imagination. Corporations use stock to make boneheaded acquisitions that make our share of the company worth relatively less. Brokerage firms rake in high underwriting commissions on companies they recommend to their customers. We the investors continue to provide the fuel for this ongoing plunder of our own hard-earned dollars by continuing to believe that the potential rewards of investing in the market more than offset the risk.

STRATEGIES FOR DEALING WITH UNCERTAINTY

The primary objective of an intelligent investment strategy should be to preserve capital and build upon it at a consistent, moderate rate in both bull and bear markets. Our personal definition of risk is simple and understandable: we don't want to lose money. But many of us are shooting at the wrong target.

Beating the market averages or matching the market is a common objective of equity mutual funds and investment advisers who seek to justify their own existence. Many of us buy into the industry's definition of risk, which views a 20 percent loss in a market that is down 25 percent as a success. This makes no sense!

Part II develops a unique but sensible means of handling investment risk. Even though the risks of investing in the stock market are tremendous, it still may provide superior returns relative to other investment options. Ideally, we could time the market and be invested during the boom times and on the sidelines during the bust times. However, since it's impossible to time the market, we need another way to deal with investment risk.

Investment advisers have traditionally dealt with stock market risk by diversification, asset allocation, and a long-term outlook. These strategies help to reduce risk when investing in equities but do not eliminate it. But are investments in equities a sensible way to provide for the future? Not when there are alternatives that allow us to participate in market gains while protecting our investment principal. We can avoid unprotected investments in the market by transferring the risk of loss to a third party.

Most of us use this technique when we purchase comprehensive and collision coverage on our automobiles. We assure that our home is protected against loss by perils we hope never happen, such as fire or natural disasters. Yet we rarely consider transferring the risk on our stock-related investments, which are subject to a long list of hazards. In addition to the dangers discussed in Part I, these hazards include political, economic, and business factors that also increase uncertainty and our chance of loss.

MAXIMIZING RETURNS WHILE MINIMIZING RISK

Part III reviews protected investments and how they work to safeguard our principal while providing a return that is tied to the market. Protected investments include market-linked certificates of deposit, market-linked notes, equity-index annuities, and equity-linked life insurance. Our principal is guaranteed and/or insured by major financial institutions that are able to provide these assurances. Our risk of loss in the stock market is effectively transferred to a third party.

For most people, the bulk of their financial investments are held in retirement plans, including 401(K), 403(B), and IRA plans. Incorporating protected investments into these plans will increase the probability of securing a comfortable retirement. A separate chapter is devoted to the challenges of investing for retirement.

Part III also addresses the problems and issues outlined in Part I, as well as key corrective actions that our society needs to consider right now.

EXTREMIST VIEW OR LOGICAL CONCLUSION?

At first glance it may seem like this book promotes alarmist thinking with an extremist view of avoiding stocks and mutual funds in favor of more predictable and controllable investment options. However, it all boils down to a simple matter of evaluating risk versus reward. When you consider all the facts, it is just plain common sense that most people should avoid unprotected investments in the stock market.

PART I

THE AVERAGE PERSON SHOULD STEER CLEAR OF STOCKS—HERE'S WHY

CHAPTER ONE

THE STOCK MARKET
CAN WE WIN AT THIS GAME?

*The investor's chief problem—and even his worst enemy—
is likely to be himself.*

BENJAMIN GRAHAM, FATHER OF VALUE INVESTING,

SECURITY ANALYSIS, 1934

INDIVIDUAL INVESTOR PERFORMANCE VS. THE MARKET

MANY MODERN-DAY investors have become like crazed gamblers, risking their nest eggs and retirement money on visions of a chance at 20 percent-plus returns on their investment portfolios. Most of them don't even take the time to read a financial statement, yet they scamper to brokerage firms and mutual funds, surrendering every spare cent they can on a stock market system few of them understand. Greed, advertising, and peer pressure have lured them into a terrifying real-life game with sky-high stakes of fortune or poverty.

That's gambling.

Have investors forgotten that stocks do not exist just to give us a lottery ticket to future riches? Stocks finance the agendas of business and their corporate executives. It's a system run by professionals who spend a lifetime mining riches, at times contrary to the letter of the law. In the end, when the vein is dry, the gold is in their account; the fool's gold is what's left in our portfolios.

Who's Winning, Really—the Cold, Hard Facts

When it comes to making investment decisions, as Benjamin Graham said, the individual investor is often his or her own worst enemy. In June 2001 the research firm Dalbar Inc., of Boston, released a study entitled "Quantitative Analysis of Investor Behavior." The study examined real investor returns from January 1984 through December 2000. It found that the individual equity mutual fund investor realized an annual return of 5.32 percent compared to 16.3 percent for the S&P 500 index. In addition, the study found mutual fund investments were retained for an average of only 2.6 years.[1]

The severe underperformance relative to the S&P 500 index and the frequent trading indicate very poor timing on the part of the individual investor. Dalbar previously conducted similar studies in 1994 and 1998. The 1998 study found that the return of the S&P 500 was five and one half times greater than the return earned by the average investor. All three studies showed that the typical mutual fund investor earned inferior returns to the S&P 500 as well as the average mutual fund.

Money magazine published a study by Charles Trzcinka, professor of finance at Indiana University, in June 2002. This fascinating analysis described the difference between the returns that mutual funds report and those of the average investor in the funds. According to Professor Trzcinka, the average mutual fund gained 5.7 percent during the four-year period of the study between 1998 and 2001, while the average investor earned only 1.0 percent. The study analyzed the returns of more than 6,900 U.S. stock mutual funds and adjusted for money that was shoveled in and yanked out during the period.

The table that follows enumerates some of the details of this unique study. The large disparity between the fund's stated returns and the amount investors actually realized was a surprise even to Professor Trzcinka. According to the professor: "The sheer magnitude of the difference we discovered between the total returns earned by mutual funds and the results captured by the average shareholder is *shocking and tragic.*"[2]

ANNUALIZED RETURN 1998–2001

MUTUAL FUND NAME	FUND RETURN	INVESTOR RETURN
FIDELITY AGGRESSIVE GROWTH	2.8%	−24.1%
VANGUARD CAP APPRECIATION	29.2%	5.2%
INVESCO DYNAMICS	7.0%	−14.4%
JANUS MERCURY	13.9%	−7.4%
FIDELITY SELECT ELECTRONICS	21.7%	−7.6%

Dalbar attributes the chasm between mutual fund and individual performance to the active investor's destructive behavioral patterns, which include a phenomenon known as *herd mentality.* These patterns involve waiting for a fund to have a few good years and then pouring in a flood of cash just before the fund reaches its peak. The investor then proceeds to ride the fund to near bottom and sells out. This is precisely opposite to the conventional investment wisdom of *buying low and selling high.*

Both the Dalbar and Trzcinka studies reached the same conclusion. The Dalbar research indicated that investors underperformed the market by approximately 67 percent. The Trzcinka study, covering a different time period, indicated investors underperformed the funds they were invested in by about 82 percent. According to an Economic Policy Institute briefing paper, it will take the average household over thirty years to recover the wealth lost in 2000 and 2001 from market declines![3] With these miserable statistics, does it make sense for the individual investor to be playing this dangerous game of stock market investing?

■ ■ ■

The *Journal of Finance* published a study in 2001 that was appropriately titled "Massively Confused Investors Making Conspicuously Ignorant Choices."[4] Befuddled investors spend thousands of dollars purchasing stocks by mistake because they confuse company symbols. According to Harvard researcher Michael Rashes, investors often know so little about the stocks they buy and sell that they simply guess at what they think the ticker symbol might be and begin trading. Most would agree that this is not the best investment strategy.

Assuming investors correctly identify the desired stocks, they still must bear enormous market risk. Consider the period March 2000 through May 2002. It was common for techno-buffs to lose 40 percent or more of their portfolio value. The family of Janus Funds, a favorite of individual investors, was extremely hard hit. Janus Fund lost 46 percent; Janus Twenty fell 61 percent; and Janus Worldwide dropped 49 percent during this period.

Many investors took a fatalistic approach. The common mind-set became "What can I do? Everyone is losing money in the market. Well, I'm not going to worry. I have ten years to make it back."

Losing money in any market is neither inevitable nor universal. Moreover, depending upon the timing, the investor may not have the luxury of waiting ten years to "make it back." Short-term losses can have devastating long-term impacts if money is needed for living expenses and is no longer there. The next ten years are just as subject to declines as the last ten. Attempting to beat the market always means taking on risk and can lead to the gut-wrenching possibility of further loss.

The primary objective of an intelligent investment strategy should be to *preserve capital* and build on it at a consistent, moderate rate in both bull and bear markets. But don't expect to hear this kind of advice from the professional money managers on Wall Street.

PROFESSIONAL INVESTMENT MANAGERS VS. THE MARKET

Investment performance is a zero-sum game. For every investor who beats the market, another one underperforms it. You would expect that the hardworking, skilled professional investors with substantial resources at their command would gain at the expense of the unskilled individual investor and consistently beat the market averages. But this is not the case.

The Professional Investment Manager vs. a Blindfolded Monkey

In 1985 Dr. Burton G. Malkiel's epic book, *A Random Walk Down Wall Street,* rocked the professional investment world. Dr. Malkiel, a professor of economics at Princeton University, concluded it was difficult, if not impossible, for the average active professional money manager to consistently beat an index of stocks, which by definition is unmanaged. His book was not a welcome addition to the library of financial literature—at least not from the perspective of Wall Street. Stockbrokers, investment analysts, portfolio managers, and other financial professionals pride themselves on their abilities to make money by implementing their exceptional understanding of the logic and rationality of the stock markets. It's what a good part of the investment industry is based upon—the marketing of expert advice.

Dr. Malkiel detonated this myth by exploring the limitations of active financial management. An academician, he used his scholarly tools to demonstrate that individual stock prices move randomly and are totally unpredictable in the short run. He reasoned that investors would be better off buying an unmanaged index of stocks in lieu of using a professional or trying to manage the funds themselves. According to Malkiel, "A blindfolded monkey throwing darts" could theoretically pick stocks as well as a financial professional.[5]

■ ■ ■

The disappointing performance of actively managed mutual funds by Wall Street professionals is well documented. Charles Ellis reports, in *Winning the Losers Game,* over 75 percent of professionally managed funds underperformed the S&P 500 index for the twenty-five-year period ending in 1997.[6] Max Isaacman, author of *How to Be an Index Investor,* cites one analysis that showed an astounding 96 percent of professional money managers did worse than the S&P 500 index.[7]

Another study conducted by Ira Weiss, an accounting professor at Columbia Business School, reviewed U.S. fund performance for thirty-six years through December 1997. He found that diversified funds gained an average of 12 percent less per year than the S&P 500 index.[8]

Mutual fund organization Morningstar conducted research that indicated for the ten years ending December 31, 1998, the Wilshire 5000 index of most regularly traded U.S. stocks outperformed a collection of selected high-performing funds by an average of 7.2 percent.[9]

Mutual fund investors who chase after managers who beat the market odds are likely to be disappointed. A top-performing manager one year is not likely to excel in the following year.[10] In the absence of consistency, the excellent performance turned in for one period can be attributed to nothing more than sheer luck.

Investment newsletters reinforce the same message, even as they add their own layer of analytical complexity to that of the funds they select. A study by the *Hulbert Financial Digest* found that between August 1987 and the end of 1998, the average fund newsletter's model portfolio provided a return of 7.3 percent—only *one half* of the 14.1 percent return on the

Wilshire 5000 index. Only six out of fifty-five advisers did better than the market. All claimed, at least implicitly, to provide market-beating returns with their complex multilayered approaches, but precious few delivered on that promise.[11]

One reason it is extremely difficult for fund managers to beat the market is the drag on performance created by trading costs and the expenses of running a fund. Another reason is that it is virtually impossible to beat the market over time without taking on additional risk. This is why *indexing* (matching overall market performance) has grown so rapidly, and now accounts for an estimated 23 percent of institutional equity investing in the United States, even though it offers no protection against loss.[12]

A HISTORICAL PERSPECTIVE ON THE MARKET

In•vest•ment *n.* the outlay of money usually for income or profit.
  Merriam-Webster's Dictionary

What Happened to the Blue-Chip Stock Era?

To this day my father, 77, still works for the same company, lives in the same house, and has been married for almost fifty years. The son of a coal miner and a survivor of the Depression, Ed Winslow Sr., sticks to insured investments, absolutely refusing to get into stock market gambles. You can tell by his suit, his punctuality, and his unswerving level-headedness that he has a savings account, a life insurance policy, and a retirement plan. He hasn't changed his philosophy one iota—not even during the roaring bull market of the late 1990s.

Throughout his life, Dad invested one way—U.S. government-backed bonds, FDIC insured CDs, and bank accounts; and, as he got older and more adventurous, U.S. agency-backed mortgages. Of course, before investing in anything, his first priority was paying off the mortgage and being debt free.

So he's still at it, now working part-time as an accountant and making conservative investments. The global economy is changing like a kaleidoscope around him—the times have changed—but he sets his steady course, unaffected.

■ ■ ■

How did we go from the secure, sleepy years of Eisenhower to today's dazzling casino of options, futures, and stock market gambles? Can we even refer to ourselves as "investors"?

Stocks and mutual funds don't match *Webster's* definition of investment. The description would have to be tweaked to include the disclaimer that your dollar does indeed offer the potential for profit—even great profit—but only at a high risk of loss. If there is a possibility of losing money, we are talking speculation, not investment.

There are no guarantees that stocks will offer profitable returns in the future—even in the long run. It only takes one gigantic loss to collapse a dream. Many ordinary Americans trusted Enron with their retirement dreams. Tragically, they ended up with a nightmare.

■ ■ ■

When the biotech craze started in the late 1990s, everyone—investors and analysts alike—saw huge potential. Ordinary middle-class Americans, motivated by a fear of being left out and hoping to make some fast bucks, bought into the get-rich-quick promises of this industry. All told, billions of dollars were poured into brand-new companies with no more than a concept and a rough business plan. Most of these companies, giddy with newfound wealth, burned through the investors' money with outrageous salaries and outlandish benefits, and either went out of business or were picked up for pennies on the dollar by more savvy corporations.

Wall Street and its investors were not focused on current profits but on the *potential* for future profits. Many small phar-

maceutical and biotechnology companies had little or no current sales but had a "promising" product in the pipeline that
was expected to have a shot at commercial success.

Earnings and profitability might have been years away and
for that matter might never occur. Nevertheless, corporations
hired public relations firms to put a positive spin on whatever
was happening, even when the financial statements indicated
there was nothing to crow about. Promised day and night by
news, television, the Internet, mail, and cold calls from
strangers about the fabulous wealth to be gained in the stock
market, who wouldn't be green with greed?

Well, there is no free lunch. If you are a conservative
investor, you must avoid individual stocks and equity mutual
funds. It's of the utmost importance to protect your principal
while earning a return on your investment. If your principal is
at risk, you are not an investor, you're a gambler.

How Long Is Long Enough?

It's interesting to review past market returns as a basis for esti-
mating future returns. For the 101 years ending in 2000, the
world stock markets were up an inflation-adjusted 5.2 percent
annually with the U.S. figure at 6.7 percent.[13] But who lives
101 years? And at what point during that 101 years do you cash
out your portfolio to pay for college tuition, retirement shortfalls, prescriptions, or nursing home care?

The money manager's mantra, especially when the market
drops, is "Hold on, don't panic; the good times are coming
back, we're investing for the long term." What investor hasn't
heard this? It's an article of faith that a representative sample of
stocks, if held for the long run, can't fail to pay off. Under the
buy-and-hold theory, investors owning stocks always *expect* to
do better relative to other investments, versus—perish the
thought—*going stockless!*

The number one rule in Michael Sivy's book, *Rules of Investing,* is that on average "you can't lose with blue-chip stocks if

you plan to hold them for twenty years."[14] Jane Bryant Quinn, in *Making the Most of Your Money*, says: "I like stocks if the holding period is 4 or 5 years. I love stocks for holding periods of 10 years or more."[15] This common advice is spread throughout every form of media. The magazine *Women in Business* had an article about what to do when bad news strikes your stocks. According to the article, the first rule was not to panic. "You will most likely want to maintain your long-term, buy and hold outlook. In fact you may even want to buy more shares."[16]

But are ten or even twenty years long enough? The answer may surprise you.

No one knows what the future holds, but the chart below illustrates how the bear market of 1973–1974 wiped out all of the spectacular gains of the 1960s and took the market back to 1961 levels.

S & P 500

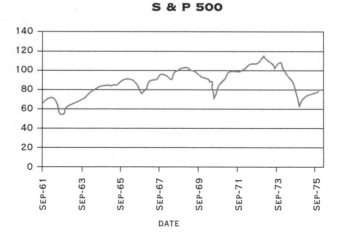

DATE

The bear market of 1929–1932 wiped out all of the gains of the previous 33 years. An investment at the top of the market in 1929 had to be held until 1954 before showing a hint of profit. History shows us that the market can be extremely volatile and is definitely not for the faint of heart.

■ ■ ■

Using the past performance of the stock market as a basis for predicting future performance is commonly done, even though the world is a much different place than it was just ten years ago. The ups and downs of the market can be expected to become even more dramatic in the future as the pace of change grows faster and faster. When news, good or bad, is instantaneous, so is the investor's reaction.

Fickle Figures of Fate

There is a statistical anomaly that occurs when year-to-year results are reported for volatile up-and-down stocks and mutual funds in today's market. This quirk of mathematics makes the gains seem bigger and the losses smaller than they really are. For example, a 50 percent loss requires a 100 percent gain to recover.

Consider a stock or fund that reports being up 20 percent the first year, down 20 percent the second, up 40 percent the third, and down 40 percent in year four. At first glance it appears that the investment will break even at the end of four years, but this is not the case. The end results of these performance figures are quite surprising:

	% GAIN	VALUE
BASE YEAR		$1,000
YEAR 1	+20	1,200
YEAR 2	−20	960
YEAR 3	+40	1,344
YEAR 4	−40	806

The above calculation shows that an investment of $1,000 would actually end up being down by approximately 19 percent. This investor would have experienced a wild roller-coaster ride, with exhilarating ups and breathtaking downs, only to end up below where he or she started four years earlier.

Now consider the actual figures reported by the NASDAQ composite index, which reached a level of 5048.62 on March 10, 2000. This was a whopping 256 percent increase from its closing level of 1419.12 on October 8, 1998, in merely nineteen months. Exciting times indeed! However, the fall from the high of 5048.62 to 1423.19 on September 21, 2001, equals *72 percent*, which coincidentally also took approximately one and one half years. The 256 percent gain *sounds* like it more than offsets the 72 percent loss, but the money in your wallet is just as thin as when you began.

The investor who bought in at the low in 1998 and held for the three years had a quick ride to nowhere. A $100,000 investment would have increased to $356,000 and gone right back down to the $100,000 level, all within a three-year period. The 256 percent increase was wiped out by the decrease of 72 percent. When the professional money manager starts to tout percentage increases by year, beware!

■ ■ ■

Historically, buying and holding a mutual fund or stock over a long period of time used to be the time-tested thing to do. As every investor today knows, that clearly is no longer true. Such a strategy certainly didn't help the NASDAQ index investor between 1998 and 2001.

The new investment strategies and products discussed later in this book allow for the capture of all or a portion of a gain in an up cycle while providing principal protection in a down period. This is the *only* way it makes sense to have an investment that is tied to corporate stock and the market.

Why? What has changed?

Integrity Losing Out to Illusion

For the last decade, the *new* bottom line for the corporation has been to increase the stock price in as short a time as possible. It is the measure, the countermeasure, the golden rule, and the ruthless rod by which a corporation will thrive or die. Image, marketability, and great expectations are what drive a stock price higher—not necessarily real production numbers and actual service. The purveyors of that image are the very few, at the very top, who reap obscene monetary benefits by creating a utopian aura of corporate health, growth, prosperity, and vision.

While common investors were basking in the glow of their inflated portfolio, Arthur Levitt, former chairman of the Securities and Exchange Commission, foresaw the dark undercurrents of market manipulation. He noted in a 1998 speech that executives were facing pressure to deliver steady earnings each quarter. "Managing may be giving way to manipulation; integrity may be losing out to illusion," he warned.[17]

How is the illusion created?

Dubbed "earnings management," the practice of tailoring earnings to meet market expectations has become part and parcel of doing business on Wall Street.[18] In other words, today's executive woos us with a kind of financial wizardry. Numbers are coaxed and massaged and manipulated until they present the desired picture. Losses are reported with the connotation: "Let's put the bad times behind us; a great future lies ahead." Huge losses can be hidden beneath a complex accounting game.

Aided by the hard-earned dollars of millions of Americans, today's large corporation has become a wealthy wonderland for some CEOs and their inner circle, who charge admission to their illusory world via purchases of common stock. Most average investors don't even bother reading the annual reports and their massaged numbers. They are captivated by the magical mantra constantly drumming in their ears—*the market always goes up in the long run.* We are like the three monkeys. We see not. We hear not. We speak not.

■ ■ ■

"Greed, . . . for lack of a better word, is good," says Gordon Gekko, a fictitious corporate executive in the 1987 movie *Wall Street.* Gekko's speech caught the spirit of an era that continues barreling along today. In theory, when the self-interest of top executives is aligned with the investors, companies should do well. The profit motive is the driver and is needed at all levels, including individual investors and management, for the system to work. It's the underlying fuel for our economic system. But when it gets out of control and becomes raw unrestrained greed, a continuing uninterrupted cascade of scandals can result, ranging from insider trading to outright fraud.

The Crushing Weight of the Pyramid

The pyramid ranks the parties in order of their potential returns from the stock market game. At the top of the pyramid is the party that takes on the least amount of investment risk but receives the highest potential rewards. The average investor on the bottom of the pyramid takes on the greatest amount of risk but receives the lowest return.

Motivated by greed and potential profit, individuals have bought into the scheme in droves. According to Morningstar, the number of mutual fund accounts leap-frogged from 8 million in 1976, to 46 million in 1986, to 227 million in 1999. Individual brokerage accounts, hopping on for the ride, soared. We have given our unwarranted trust and blind faith to a system that holds our financial future captive solely on the basis of a long-held belief that common stock is the best long-term investment choice we have at our disposal. So we hold our breath and hope for the best.

INFORMATION, TRADING COSTS, AND TURNOVER
Information Overload

We are inundated with millions of pieces of data each day. The advent of the Internet makes it possible to have data and information at our fingertips in a matter of seconds. There is so much to absorb that scientists are studying ways humans can deal with the stress of an overworked brain. Preliminary findings suggest that the burnout sensation that comes with information overload results from fatigue in specific brain regions. Burnout is the signal that says you can't take in more information in this part of your brain until you've had a chance to sleep.[19] Metaphorically speaking, as a nation we are suffering from real-time market overload exhaustion.

We didn't have to worry about information overload a century ago. People were grateful for any kind of information or news they could get. Sometimes it would take days to get news from certain countries. Timely corporate investment news such as earnings reports would be disseminated through brokers. There were no email alerts, online quotes, and real-time trading viewed on CNBC. Naps were an enjoyable pastime, not a neurological necessity.

Commission-Free Trading

As the speed and quantity of investment information has accelerated, the costs of trading have plunged. Today, an investor can buy or sell any number of shares of stock for as little as ten dollars per transaction or less. These same transactions, done through a full-commission broker, might cost thousands of dollars.

Excessive Portfolio Turnover

The combination of cheap trading costs and availability of superfast information has encouraged many investors to speculate in stocks, enabling a lot of buying and selling that in the old days would have been cost prohibitive. Now the trading cost is negligible compared to the transaction size. The increased turnover resulting from the shorter time period investors hold stock isn't of any help to the average investor. In fact, studies show that the more investors trade, the less they earn.[20]

Increased turnover creates higher volatility and risk. The convenience of getting online, and at the push of a button trading a stock, gives the whole investment process the feel of a computer game, which is fine entertainment if the money is simulated. But we're talking real money. This is money being saved for the new car, the kids' college education, the daughter's wedding, and our own retirement.

■ ■ ■

Today's investor is at a crossroads. The strategy of buying stock and holding it for a long period of time has worked in the past. Many of us have made and lost money, some of it substantial, in the stock market. Even a quick review of recent history shows a trail littered with wild ups and downs. But the big question is: What does the future hold?

One of the keys to understanding the market, and our place in it, is to look at the psychology that drives it—and us.

CHAPTER TWO

FAITH IN OURSELVES
THE IRRATIONAL BEHAVIOR
OF INVESTORS

*Man is not to be comprehended in terms of sophisticated economic
laws in which his innate ferocity and creativity are smothered under a
cloak of rationalization. He is better dealt with in the less flattering
but more fundamental vocabulary of the anthropologist or the psychol-
ogist: a creature of strong and irrational drives, credulous, untutored,
and ritualistic. Economists should leave aside flattering fictions and
find out why man actually behaves as he does.*

THORSTEIN VEBLEN, *AMERICAN ECONOMIST (1857–1929)*

THE BEHAVIOR OF INDIVIDUAL
INVESTORS

DO PEOPLE ACT rationally when making decisions about
their investments? The connection between money and
motive can leave us wide open and vulnerable to some very
questionable investment strategies. Most economic and financial theory is based on the premise that people do act logically
and consider all available information in the decision-making
process. However, a surprising amount of evidence exists indicating that human beings show repeated patterns of incon-
sistency, irrationality, and incompetence when faced with
decisions or choices that deal with uncertainty.

For example, psychologists say the technology stock bubble
that peaked in early 2000 was due to irrational overconfidence
in these companies. Perceived as exciting and ripe for growth,

these stocks generated investor pleasure as well as pride in their ownership. This was the hidden hook that lured and caught many little fish investors.

The investment industry asserted that technology stocks were benefiting from a factor known as *momentum investing,* a practice in which investors pile into a stock or sector simply because it is going up. Although the Wall Street explanation sounds more scientific, it acknowledges the herd mentality that occurs with investors because of psychological and social factors.

A relatively new field in psychology known as behavioral finance attempts to explain and better understand the psyche of the investor and how emotions influence the decision-making process.

One of the pioneers of *behavioral finance* was the late Amos Tversky, professor of psychology at Stanford University. Tversky found that individuals are much more distressed by prospective losses than they are happy with equivalent gains. Faced with a sure gain, many investors become risk averse, but faced with sure loss, investors become risk takers. Mind-forged handcuffs bind us to our mistakes. Some economists have concluded that investors typically consider the loss of one dollar twice as painful as the pleasure from a one dollar gain.[1] Most people are unwilling to realize their losses, and they assume *additional* risk in an attempt to avoid such losses. This often results in further damage to the investment portfolio.

I've found that investors hesitate to liquidate investments that have gone down in value, even when there is a logical, rational argument for selling. Perhaps it is the pain that Tversky refers to when a loss is actually realized. I've also seen the opposite occur when an investment has been such a good performer that investors won't consider selling. Perhaps they fear the possibility of missing out on further gains. They forget that a gain is not a gain until it is realized. This mentality is so strong in some investors that they become paralyzed, unable to make any rational decisions concerning their investments. Meir Statman, professor of behavioral finance at Santa Clara University, calls this phenomenon the "fear of regret."

Regret is the pain we feel when we find, too late, that other choices would have led to better outcomes. It is the ache of investors who bought a stock or fund only to see its value plummet. Investors with unrealized losses often grow increasingly convinced that, in time, their stocks will roar back and their choices will be vindicated. They desperately linger on the notion that a loss is not really a loss until it is realized. Unable to admit to error, many an investor has ended up holding stock in a bankrupt company.

The same behavior applies to forecasters who stake out strong bullish or bearish positions. Once an opinion on a stock is given publicly, analysts or forecasters hesitate to change their stated position.[2]

According to Professor Statman, people tend to feel sorrow and grief after making an error in judgment. Investors deciding whether to sell a security are emotionally affected by whether the security was bought at more or less than the current price. Perhaps it's the syndrome of "I'd rather be right than rich" that keeps the investor in a bad stock, or facing the embarrassment that your accountant will see, in black and white, your failure in the market.

Another way investors cope with portfolio losses is simply to ignore them. In an article entitled "When It Hurts Too Much to Look," the *Wall Street Journal* reported that in good times people enjoy looking at their investment statements, but in bad, many let them pile up unopened and unread. That is because investors are afflicted with loss aversion and come up with elaborate mental constructs, such as "it's only a paper loss," to reduce their pain.

"Not opening the envelope takes the suspension of disbelief one step further," says Hersh Shefrin, a professor of finance and economics at Santa Clara University. "It makes financial reality less salient. There are many studies that show that out of sight really can be out of mind."[3]

To avoid the pain and regret of an independent bad decision, many investors follow the crowd, buying the media's latest darlings. It is easier to go down with the ship along with everyone else who bought a ticket on the same *Titanic* stock cruise.

■ ■ ■

The old adage "the pride goeth before the fall" could not have stood the test of time without our help. A fascinating aspect of human behavior is that people are overconfident in their own abilities. Investors and analysts who have some knowledge, education, or training are particularly overconfident. For example, analysts will frequently exaggerate the reliability of their forecasts. If they say it loud enough, often enough, and with absolute certainty, they seem to believe the market will hear and conform itself to their mental prowess. Tversky calls this phenomenon the "illusion of validity." Tversky asserts that "People are prone to experience much confidence in highly fallible judgment. Like other perceptual and judgmental errors, the illusion of validity persists even when its illusionary character is recognized."[4]

Richard Thayler of the University of Chicago conducted an experiment on human behavior in his classroom. He concluded that people are more willing to take risks and gamble when they're ahead on a stock. When the investment has dropped in value they become more conservative. Many people have similar feelings when they go to a casino. Thayler describes this as the "house money" effect.[5]

People hear what they want to hear. During the dot-com frenzy, many investors listened to the analysts projecting ever-increasing share prices for Internet companies. Yet there were plenty of quicksand warnings posted: overvaluation, lack of profits, unsound expansion strategies. But those warnings went unheeded by scores of investors.

People tend to fall prey to what psychologists call a *confirmation bias*—a kind of mental filter that takes in information consistent with a person's beliefs and screens out inconsistent or conflicting information.[6] This problem of human psychology is not unique to the investment field. Robert Park, a physicist, discussing the faulty research on electromagnetic fields states, "It's not deliberate fraud . . . people are awfully good at fooling themselves. They're so sure they know the answer that they don't want to confuse people with ugly looking data."[7]

Equally as perplexing as ignoring facts they don't want to hear, the frequent trading by investors has puzzled many researchers. The buyer and seller in a speculative trade both believe they are acting on superior information. Like the next person to walk up to a recently vacated slot machine, they believe *their* nickel will cause the machine to hit the jackpot. People often make buy or sell decisions on information they believe to be superior, when in fact it is not, and has actually been debunked by the market itself. They look at their own decision-making process as superior and rational while feeling that everyone else is out to lunch.

Terrance Odean of the University of California–Davis analyzed trading records for 10,000 accounts at a large discount brokerage firm. Professor Odean found that on average, purchased stocks performed worse than the stocks that were sold. The investor would have been better off leaving the portfolio alone. This was true even when trading was not motivated by liquidity demands, tax-loss selling, portfolio rebalancing, or a move to lower-risk securities—in other words, when it was purely an investment decision.

In addition, he found that on any given day an investor is two times more likely to sell a stock that has gone up rather than one that has gone down. Professor Odean concluded that excessive trading by investors contributes to their underperformance and is caused by factors that include overconfidence, too much reliance on outside information such as analyst reports, and a reluctance to sell losing positions.[8] Essentially, these investors are holding their losses and selling their profits. They'll keep trading until they get a losing stock, and then keep it.

Day Trading—the Minute-by-Minute Market

The technology revolution and the Internet, along with the 1990s bull market, made day trading part of the American culture. Day traders attempt to make profits on small changes in the prices of stocks. They are known as *day* traders because they are taught to close out their positions by the end of the day. Day trading firms provide computer terminals and sophisticated software to track stock prices via dedicated-line access to the market. Only a few years prior, this type of system was limited to brokerage firms. Today, anyone can become a day trader.

In August 1999 *Time* magazine published an article entitled "Day Trading: It's a Brutal World," which estimated that the number of folks who quit their jobs to become full-time day traders was about 5,000. But if you add those who trade online at home or between meetings at the office, there are as many as 5 million. The technology made it possible, and the bull market made it irresistible.

The article quoted Jake Bernstein, author of *The Compleat Day Trader*, who said that only about 15 percent of those who take up day trading make money at it. Many lose big because they don't have the discipline to sell immediately when a stock moves against them, or they sell too soon when a stock moves their way. "If you have a lot at risk you are prone to acting on emotion," Bernstein said, "and emotional decisions are likely to be bad decisions."

A successful trader has to be able to stay calm while absorbing painful losses, according to Ari Kiev, a psychiatrist and trading coach also quoted in the *Time* article: "You start to lose, and you try to make it back, but you lose more. You lose the college money and then the rent money. That activates feelings of inadequacy, failure, and catastrophe. You start blaming everyone but yourself. It's very destructive."[9]

The interesting thing about the day trading phenomenon is how attractive it seems to the average person. Even when the risks are outlined and understood, many people forge ahead believing that they are more intelligent than everybody else. In addition, the element of high risk adds excitement to the process. I had three clients who took a portion of their wealth and did day trading on their own during 1999 despite my cautionary counsel. Two of the three lost everything, while the third was down by 90 percent. All of this occurred in a matter of less than six months.

What Type of Investor Are You?

Individuals and institutions often hire full-service broker/adviser professionals to manage equity investments. Overwhelmed by the thousands of investment possibilities, such investors seek help with the decision-making process. Researchers theorize that the investment adviser plays a very important role in the process—that of the scapegoat.

In the book *Fortune and Folly: The Wealth and Power of Institutional Investing*, the authors conclude that officers and directors of large pension plans hire outside investment managers for no other reason than to provide cover in the event of underperformance. If the fund tanks, the financial adviser is fired; if it flourishes, the directors' wisdom and the financial manager's acumen are lauded. Of course, this same logic holds true for the individual investor. Individual investors will congratulate themselves on their ability to pick an adviser who shows good performance and use the adviser as the scapegoat for poor performance.[10]

■ ■ ■

In many ways, individuals are unique and exhibit their own distinctive behavior. But according to the banking industry, individual investors can be divided into three categories. An investor is either *control oriented,* making all the decisions and not needing any advice or direction, or *passive,* handing over the keys to the kingdom to a third party. Between those two extremes are the *participative* investors, who seek professional advice but remain involved in the decision-making process. Factors of personality, financial wealth, and age provide important overlays to this categorization process.

For example, investors tend to be more control oriented in earlier years, which makes sense. They have discretionary income; they're more on top of their game intellectually and energywise; they're climbing the corporate ladder. But in retirement, investors often become passive. They'd rather be on the golf course or reading a good book than poring over the intricacies of annual reports.[11]

When it comes to gender, who are the real risk takers—men or women? No surprises here. *Psychographics*—the interconnection between demographics and psychological perspective—has proven that women tend to be more risk averse than men and are comfortable being passive investors. Marketing studies also indicate that men tend to be more active as well as control oriented and enjoy taking risks. But it has also been proven that women generally show superior investment performance relative to the opposite sex.

Bailard, Biel and Kaiser, an investment advisory firm, divides investors into five categories. Adventurers are the risk takers and are particularly difficult to advise. Celebrities like to be where the action is and are easy prey for fast-talking salespeople. Individualists tend to avoid extreme risk, do their own research, and try to act rationally. Guardians are typically older, more careful, and more risk averse. Straight Arrows fall between the other four personalities and are typically well balanced.[12]

Under this categorization, the Adventurers and Celebrities "play" the market as a source of entertainment and realize that it is just another form of gambling. It's the Individualists, the Guardians, and the Straight Arrows who feel they are forced to play the game and unwittingly take on much more risk than they may realize. They are especially irritated with the fluctuations of the market and would love to have a better way to invest.

THE MADNESS OF CROWDS
Market Mania

Yale University economist Robert Shiller wrote a book entitled *Irrational Exuberance,* named after Alan Greenspan's memorable phrase in a speech given in December 1996. In painstaking detail, Shiller describes how the roaring bull market of the 1990s was nothing more than a speculative binge: irrational, self-propelled, and self-inflated.[13]

The astonishing run-up in prices had very little to do with earnings or dividend growth. Instead it was a reflection of human psychology—a kind of collective belief that financial gravity did not necessarily apply. Shiller notes that these same forces of human psychology can drive the markets into a downward spiral with equal disregard for economic data.

Shiller believes that there is a *zeitgeist*—a spirit of the times—when it comes to the market, and that it is an extremely powerful force. In the late 1990s everyone may have known, at least on a subconscious level, that the market was overvalued. But no one changed his or her behavior. The behavioral power of human forces that compel people to do what they do will always triumph. If the basic force is optimism or greed, the markets will remain exuberant. If the basic force is pessimism or fear, then no amount of earnings or dividend increases will assuage it.[14]

According to Shiller, human behavior is what drives prices, and you can throw the *efficient-market theory* out the window. The *efficient-market theory* asserts that financial prices accurately reflect all public information at all times. In other words, stocks are correctly priced at all times. This theory is to the economics and the financial profession what the belief in God is to the Catholic Church: an article of faith. Shiller insists that this fundamental assumption by the traditional financial community is totally wrong.

Shiller's insight seems to fit what anyone can observe of today's market. Stocks fluctuate up and down wildly based on the latest press release or international crisis or presidential speech. Logically, each publicly traded company is producing the same product and service as it was just minutes before the news, but the *reaction* of the investor is irrationally euphoric or catastrophically morose. Internet technology has made it too convenient for investors to make rash decisions based upon their emotional reactions.

■ ■ ■

In 1895 a French sociologist named Gustav Le Bon authored a book called *The Crowd: A Study of the Popular Mind*.[15] Le Bon's book was inspired by the political and social turmoil of his times. He asserted that the crowd was not driven by rational argument but by its spinal cord. It responded solely to emotional appeals and was incapable of thought or reason. Leaders of a group of people, he proposed, need to appeal not to logic but to unconscious motivation.

Le Bon's book was written with the working class in mind, but by the 1920s his ideas were applied to virtually everyone. Almost no one is seen as capable of rational thought. The most efficient way to win hearts and minds is through emotional appeals. The modern industry of public relations is based upon this premise, and it applies to the politics of democratic government as well as to the investment industry where people are voting with their money.

Survey research, polling, and focus groups are all built around the science of tallying that emotional reaction. Since the 1920s this quantification of public feeling has gained credibility because media and corporate and political leaders give it credence. Today we see the public expressing itself as a kind of statistical applause track to the headlines of the day.[16]

■ ■ ■

In 1841 Charles Mackay wrote his classic work on crowd psychology, speculative bubbles, and manias. Entitled *Extraordinary Popular Delusions and the Madness of Crowds,* Mackay wrote, "Money, again, has been a cause of the delusions of the multitudes. Sober nations have all at once become desperate gamblers, and risked almost their existence upon the turn of a piece of paper. Men, it has well been said, think in herds; it will be seen that they go mad in herds, while they only recover their senses slowly, and one by one."[17]

All of the idiosyncrasies of individual investors can be magnified, creating dramatic bubbles of intense speculative activity. This is not peculiar to this age. There have been many financial bubbles since the publication of Mackay's book in 1841. There was the great U.S. stock market bubble of the 1920s; the Japanese stock market and real estate bubble of the late 1980s; and the technology/Internet company bubble of the late 1990s, just to name a few.

John Kenneth Galbraith outlined the common denominators of past bubbles and manias in his 1993 book, *A Short History of Financial Euphoria.* They might be summarized as follows:

- *There are those who are persuaded that some new price-enhancing circumstance is in control, and they expect the market to stay up and go up, perhaps indefinitely.*
- *Those involved with the speculation are experiencing an increase in wealth. . . . No one wishes to believe that this is fortuitous or undeserved; all wish to think that it is the result of their own superior insight or intuition. The very*

increase in values thus captures the thoughts and minds of those being rewarded.

- *It is said that [those who express doubt] are unable, because of defective imagination or other mental inadequacy, to grasp the new and rewarding circumstances that sustain and secure the increase in values.*
- *The speculative episode always ends not with a whimper but with a bang.*[18]

In the late 1990s, after these prophetic words were written, we experienced financial euphoria followed by a period of despair that laid many investment portfolios to waste.

> *Those who do not learn from history are doomed to repeat the mistakes of history.*
>
> GEORGE SANTAYANA,
> POET AND PHILOSOPHER (1863–1952)

INVESTING OR GAMBLING?

From my perspective, the stock market is just a game, little more than a gambling casino, a complicated amusement that is virtually impossible to beat over the long run. Why then do so many people play the game?

Some games are purely games of chance. Rolling dice takes absolutely no skill, and the outcome is based solely on luck. However, some card players are genuine professionals, and the outcome depends on skill as well as luck. The successful gambling professionals use laws of probability to their advantage.

People play the stock market game because they feel that they can beat the competition (other investors) through a combination of skill and luck. Whether they do it themselves, place money in managed mutual funds, or have an investment adviser select equities or funds for them, the objective is to beat the market. Like it or not, these kinds of investments—conservative or risky—are a gamble. Why? *Because there is no preestablished protection against loss.* A stock portfolio *can* slide to zero.

A pervading myth—one vigorously promoted by Wall Street and corporate America but increasingly found suspect by burned investors—is that stock market investing is the only reasonable way to make money and beat inflation. But this is simply not true. We are not all trapped in some kind of investors' casino with the doors locked and Lady Luck spinning the wheels. We can recognize that stocks can seemingly go sky high as well as free-fall into oblivion depending upon a wide variety of circumstances that are beyond our control. There are strategies and specific types of investments that allow investors to stop gambling with their principal yet participate in the market when it's going up. These are discussed in Parts II and III.

■ ■ ■

Why is it that since the beginning of time, gambling has been such a popular pastime and often an addiction? Everyone— from the most desperate to the most respectable—seems to engage in it.

Gambling's presence in American life is nothing new. In 1850, for instance, New York City boasted one gambling hall for every eighty-five residents. Nor is it particularly novel that state legislatures have grown addicted to lottery finance. In 1832 the revenues from lotteries that were run by eight eastern states dwarfed the federal budget by a factor of four.[19]

Today, the casino gambling industry is a $50 billion business, and it's growing. In 1988 casino gambling was legal in only two states: Nevada and New Jersey. In 1994 casinos were either authorized or operating in twenty-three states. Forty-eight states now have some form of legalized gambling (Hawaii and Utah excluded). Americans currently bet over $650 billion a year on legal gambling. The industry's take from this amounts to $250 for every American, or $750 a head for the third of the population that participates every year.

In the year 2000, over 34 million people visited Las Vegas, and 127 million more frequented casinos nationally. This was the year when Americans' spending on gambling exceeded money spent on almost all other sports and entertainment combined.[20] From 1976 to 1998 there has been a fortyfold growth in American betting. These figures do not include any consideration for the gambling that takes place in the stock market.

To attract all this business, the payoff should be great, but this is not the case, and everyone knows it. State lotteries return on average only 40 percent to 60 percent of the ticket price to bettors. Blackjack returns 99.5 percent, craps returns 98.6 percent, slot machines, 95 percent, American roulette, 94.7 percent, and pari-mutuel sports betting, 91 percent.[21]

Depending on who is counting, about one in every twenty Americans has some kind of gambling problem. The most serious addicts leave carnage in their wake—everything from domestic violence and crime to suicide. Statistics show that 5 percent of Americans buy 51 percent of all lottery tickets.[22]

■ ■ ■

Available research shows that a person's economic status tends to determine the psychological and financial meaning of gambling for that person. Higher-income people see gambling as entertainment and a way to socialize with other people. Conversely, the lower the income, the more gambling is seen as a form of investment. For the poor who have few alternative ways to invest, gambling is seen less as play and more as a serious chance to transform their lives. Additional evidence indicates that lower-income people spend a much greater percentage of their income on gambling than higher-income people.[23]

I've had numerous calls over the years from people with low income and negative to zero net worth who wanted to place a good portion, if not all, of their meager savings into a "hot tip" that they received. The "tip" was usually from a relative or coworker who received a cold call from a broker pushing a low-priced stock. I would try to counsel these people away from such a risk and recommend they use their money to pay off their 18 percent interest credit card debt. That would provide them with a guaranteed 18 percent return. Some took my advice. Others really wanted to buy that stock and do it as quickly as possible. I'm sure they found a firm to execute the transaction for them. I think most of those people would have done better at the blackjack table in Las Vegas.

People's infatuation with gambling obviously does not take into account statistics or probability to determine the odds of winning, or no one would play the game. It all comes down to the minutiae relating to human behavior. Gamblers don't care that the odds are stacked against them. As a matter of fact it presents a challenge to overcome. They have a powerful ally: Lady Luck will interpose herself between them and the laws of probability and bring forth victory.

Adam Smith, the father of capitalism and a master of the subtleties of human nature, attributed the gambler's motivation to "the overwhelming conceit which the greater part of men have of their own abilities and their absurd presumption in their own good fortune."[24] This was written over 200 years ago, but it aptly describes the overconfidence that individuals exhibit today.

FACING THE REALITY

The financial markets, including equity prices, are driven by supply and demand. This in turn is determined as a result of decisions made by human beings. These decisions are based not only on rational measures but also on a complex set of emotional factors. As a result, the market's actions are a reflection of human emotions that range from despair, gloominess, and misery to outright enthusiasm and exuberance. These feelings can turn on a dime, and consequently, so do the markets.

Studies in behavioral finance have proven that human behavior is irrational and unpredictable when it comes to money. Therefore, the task of predicting the direction of the financial markets, much less individual stocks, with a high degree of confidence will always be a formidable undertaking.

■ ■ ■

Over the years I have observed many situations in which individuals come into a large sum of money, either from an inheritance, settlement of a lawsuit, sale of a piece of property, the lottery, or any other windfall. I have seen beneficiaries at one end of the spectrum immediately dispose of everything they receive via reckless spending, lavish gifts, and so on, while others at the opposite end of the spectrum hoard every penny in a low-interest savings account. For those who place it in the market through individual stock or mutual fund purchases or even via a professional money manager, the worst thing that can happen in my opinion is that they make a quick profit. Then it seems like easy money, and it creates unwarranted confidence in themselves and the system. As a result, more money is poured in without due consideration to the risks of doing so. In the long run it's actually better for the investor to experience a loss and learn right up front the very tangible risk of playing the money game with stocks or mutual funds.

As investors we have to recognize that our individual emotional behavior can be our own worst enemy. If we can accept this rather humbling assessment, we can explore alternative investment strategies with more realistic expectations.

■ ■ ■

I think that playing the stock market game is for the 25 percent to 30 percent of individuals in this country who are avid gamblers. It's a great place to fully express the fact that you are a risk taker and that you wouldn't have it any other way. It's also more socially acceptable to brag about your keen insight in selecting a winning stock or fund than showing off the suitcase of money you won from the craps table in Vegas. If you end up losing money in the stock market, at least you can write off the loss on your personal income tax return (with certain limitations), while a loss at the casino can only be used to offset your winnings. If you are really into it, you can become a day trader or, even better, become a mutual fund manager, where you can gamble with other people's money.

What about the other 70 percent to 75 percent who are not gamblers? Many investors play the game because they know of no better alternative. They stick with the conventional wisdom. Here is a quote directly from the book *Making the Most of Your Money*, by Jane Bryant Quinn, which is representative of this conformist thinking:

> *Willingness to accept stock-market risk isn't necessarily a function of your personality. It may be a function of your knowledge. The more you learn the more you'll come to understand that long-term stockholdings aren't as risky as you thought. . . . Long term, the world has always gotten richer and stocks have always trended up. On a percentage basis, history says that you might as well invest for success.*[25]

The cheerleading on behalf of stocks as the best investment choice over the long run is epitomized by this quote from the best-selling book, *The 9 Steps to Financial Freedom,* by Suze Orman:

> *Rule number one is that to invest in the stock market . . . you must invest only money that you will not need to touch for ten years. Because, as we've seen, there has never in the history of the stock market been a ten-year period of time where stocks have not outperformed every single other investment you could have made.*[26]

It's these kinds of statements that give people a false sense of security about the stock market. Orman should consider that in September 1968 the S&P 500 index was at 102.67. In September of 1978, ten years later, the index was at 102.54. Even when you consider dividends, there would have been many better places to put money during this period of time, such as bonds and real estate.

There is a better alternative, but it took me some time to reprogram my thinking away from the accepted tradition. I was thoroughly trained to embrace this philosophy of long-term investing and its supposedly irrefutable wisdom.

CHAPTER THREE

FAITH IN CORPORATIONS
TRICKS OF THE TRADE

*The greatest management sin today is not to report a loss, but to report
a loss not expected by Wall Street.*

DAN BERNHARDT, ECONOMIST,
UNIVERSITY OF ILLINOIS

CORPORATE EARNINGS
DRIVE STOCK PRICES

STOCK PICKERS love to compare companies by analyzing
easily obtainable financial statistics. One of the most
popular measures is a simple ratio. It is calculated by dividing
the current price of a stock by its last twelve months' earnings
per share, and is commonly referred to as the price to earnings
(P/E) ratio.

Corporations with similar growth prospects usually have
similar P/E ratios. The organizations that show the best earnings within the group are going to have the highest stock price.

The market price for a share of a growth company is rarely
based on assets such as cash, land, and equipment but rather on
current earnings and expectations of future earnings. Management fully realizes this and sees it as their mission to maximize
earnings. Unfortunately there is a lot of leeway in determining
how earnings are calculated. Some companies maintain strict
and conservative accounting policies, while others stretch the
rules to the limit and beyond.

CREATIVE WAYS IN WHICH MANAGE-
MENT MANIPULATES EARNINGS

As we've seen, the higher the current earnings per share and expectations for future earnings, the higher the stock price. Regrettably, management has an overabundance of accounting tricks up their sleeves that bring into question the reliability of these earnings, even when the financial statements are audited by independent accountants. There are countless ways for unethical executives to window-dress financial reports and create a positive buzz about a company. Investors have to be watchful that they don't get stung.

Stock Option Accounting

In 1950, after weeks of horse-trading, Congress sent President Truman the Revenue Act of 1950, and on September 23 he signed it into law. Buried deep within that bill was a section amending the tax code. That change, scarcely remarked upon at the time, made it legal and practical for companies to pay employees with an interesting form of currency called the stock option.

Though stock options have been available since 1950 as a means of compensating management and employees, they really didn't become popular until the mid-1980s. This makes perfect sense since stocks essentially went nowhere from 1964 to 1984. Options during this period really didn't get management excited. But once stocks took off, companies began delivering new option packages by the truckload.

The government got involved to address the problem of excess executive compensation by passing a law that essentially states that any cash paid to an executive over $1 million annually is nondeductible unless the excess is related to performance. Corporations responded by revamping their compensation schedules to get around the $1 million ceiling.

The use of stock options as a means of compensating

employees grew exponentially in the 1990s. In theory, options sound like a great tool for giving management incentive and rewarding them for a job well done. This may possibly be true in the short run. However, over a long period of time stock options serve as a big drain on shareholders, as you will soon see.

A large corporation usually has a compensation committee that is appointed by the board of directors. This group decides on the structure and distribution of the employee stock option plan. In a company that has yet to offer its shares to the public, management and key employees will be granted options to buy the company's stock for a specified time in the future at a specified price. The price may be at pennies per share, even though the future offering price to investors will most likely be much more. A company that has already gone public will usually grant options at a price that is closer to the current market price of the stock.

Options don't require any outlay of cash by the corporation. From an accounting standpoint, exercised options are treated as additional issued common stock, which increases the capital of the organization. For example, if an employee exercises an option to buy 10,000 shares of XYZ stock at a price of $1 per share, the corporation will receive $10,000 from the issuance of stock. The company increases its cash by $10,000 and its shareholder equity by $10,000. It is irrelevant from the company's standpoint whether the current market price of the stock is $2 or $200; the accounting treatment is the same.

Of course the current market price is very relevant to the employee. If the stock is at $2, the employee has a paper profit of $10,000 on the options transaction. If the stock is at $200 per share, the paper profit increases to $1,990,000. It's considered a paper profit until the gain is actually realized when the stock is sold.

Options have become a major component of employee compensation programs for many corporations. They love it! These plans don't use corporate cash and actually serve to increase the cash of the corporation. Even though this is admittedly compensation to the employee, it isn't shown as such on the corporate books and records. Therefore corporate profits are not reduced, as they logically should be. The corporation then receives a tax deduction for the profit made by employees when they exercise the option and sell the stock within a certain period of time. From a corporate perspective, this actually increases after-tax profits.[1] The IRS views employee stock options as compensation expense, while it's not an expense when reporting results to shareholders. How's that for double-dealing? Pretty bizarre!

Today we have a situation in which some firms are admitting that, yes, there is a cost that should be recognized when giving stock options to employees and management. Yet many (mostly high-tech companies) are not conceding defeat on this issue.

The Individual Investor Finishes Last

From a corporate and employee standpoint, options are a win-win proposition. They don't cost the corporation anything, and employees have a chance of making a huge profit on their stock without the risk of investing in the stock. That's right—the option holder has the option and not the obligation to buy stock. If the stock goes up, yippee! The option holder cashes in. If the stock goes down, no money was lost. The big loser here is the long-term shareholder who has invested in the company's common stock.

A simple example illustrates this point. Suppose a company has issued 1 million shares of common stock. Let's assume that its market price is $10 per share, giving the company a total market value of $10 million. Let's also assume that the company is making a profit of $100,000 per year. Earnings per share would be 10 cents ($100,000 divided by 1 million shares outstanding). The P/E ratio would be 100 ($10 per share divided by 10 cents of earnings). The board decides to implement an employee stock option plan that allows employees to purchase up to a total of 1 million shares of stock at a price of 10 cents per share. This is a great deal, so all of the employees participate in the option. A year later the company again reports profits of $100,000. However, this time there are 2 million shares outstanding because of the option exercise. This would cause earnings per share to drop to 5 cents. If the P/E ratio remains constant at 100, the market price of the stock will be closer to $5 per share because of the dilutive effect of the option. The long-term shareholder suffers a loss of 50 percent, while the insiders see their personal net worth jump by $4.9 million. Sounds like the deck is stacked against the investor in this game!

In 1998 *Forbes* published an article, "Stock Options Are Not a Free Lunch," that covered a lot of ground. In the early 1980s the total shares allocated for management and employee stock options for the 200 largest U.S. companies amounted to less than 5 percent of shares outstanding. According to Paul Meyer and Partners, a compensation consulting firm, this figure increased to 6.9 percent in 1989. By 1997 this figure had jumped to 13.2 percent. Steven Hall at Paul Meyer said, "We used to advise companies that an allocation of 10 percent was too much dilution, but we blew through that level years ago."

By 1998 fourteen of the largest companies had stock option allocations of greater than 25 percent of shares outstanding. Some of these included Delta Air Lines, Merrill Lynch, J. P. Morgan, and Transamerica Corp.[2] Smaller organizations, especially high-tech companies, have an even greater devotion to options. There are even companies that abandoned salary altogether for their chief executives. The CEO of Oglebay Norton & Co. was compensated entirely on stock option incentives.

Defenders of stock options insist that having options encourages managers to think like owner-shareholders. This couldn't be further from the truth. Ordinary shareholders have paid for and own a stake in the company. If the stock goes up, they will benefit, but if the stock goes down, they will suffer real losses. Stock option holders get an entirely different deal. If the stock goes up, they can cash in and benefit from the increase without ever risking their own money. But if the stock price goes down, unlike purchased shares, options can be repriced downwards at a later date. If the stock goes down, the company may reduce the price on the option for the benefit of the option holder. Management could effectively run a company into the ground and grant themselves options at a lower price after the stock collapses. If the stock recovers, they make a fat profit, and if it doesn't, the option holders never had their own money at risk anyway. In either case shareholders are left holding the bag.

Ulterior Motives

Given the potential for huge rewards, it would be astonishing if all managers focused on what was best for the long-term health of the company and its shareholders. It's more likely that some executives will become obsessed with maximizing the stock price and—to the greatest extent possible—take steps to influence it. It takes a naïve view of human nature to think that some unprincipled executives won't strive to increase their personal wealth at the expense of the shareholder or anyone else who gets in their way.

The Truth Comes Out, but Who Cares?

The *Forbes* article cited earlier revealed that in 1998 economic advisory firm Smithers & Co. of London released an in-depth study of the impact of stock options on the earnings of the 100 largest U.S. companies. Their conclusion was quite an eye-opener. In 1995 corporate profits would have been on average 30 percent less than reported if options were treated as a compensation expense. In 1996 full-cost accounting for options would have resulted in 36 percent lower earnings. Many companies that were showing profits were actually operating at a loss if the accounting were done properly. Other companies, including big names such as Coca-Cola, Gillette, Sun Microsystems, and Merrill Lynch, would have seen their profits cut by more than half had they treated employee stock options as the compensation expense that they are.

Parish & Company of Portland, Oregon, in a 1998 press release about employee stock option accounting, stated the opinion that the Financial Accounting Standards Board (FASB) should report to the Securities and Exchange Commission to institute accounting reforms in order to restore confidence and stability in the global capital markets. The report stated that in fiscal year 1998 Microsoft reported net income of $4.5 billion. If the employee options were reported correctly, the company would have *lost* $2.3 billion. The same applies to Cisco Systems. A profit of $1.3 billion was reported by Cisco. Proper option accounting would cause a restatement of earnings resulting in a loss of approximately $900 million. The study concluded that although Microsoft and Cisco are believed to be leaders in their industry, they were indeed unprofitable businesses.[3]

In the mid-1990s the FASB attempted to propose a method that would account for the costs of burgeoning stock option plans on a company's financial statements. The board proposed a standard requiring companies to correctly account for option costs on their financial statements. Again, according to the *Forbes* article, Dennis Beresford, the former chair of the FASB, said, "It's hard to argue that they're any different from cash compensation or any other employee cost."

Big accounting firms and much of corporate America lobbied heavily against reforming the accounting methodology for employee stock options. The brutal battle for accounting reforms was temporarily buried in 1995 with corporate America as the victor. "The argument was: reduced earnings would translate to reduced stock prices," recalls Beresford. "People said to me, 'If we have to record a reduction in income by 40 percent, our stock will go down by 40 percent, our options will be worthless, we won't be able to keep employees. It would destroy all American business and Western civilization,'" he said.[4]

In essence, options are nothing more than a legal means of transferring wealth from shareholders to senior management and key employees of the corporation. In other words: they are a mechanism for siphoning funds from the owner-share-holders who have risked their money to the very individuals they have entrusted to mind the store.

ALICE-IN-WONDERLAND ACCOUNTING

The accounting treatment of employee stock options is only one of many controversial areas where liberal interpretation of accounting principles can lead to improper or misleading financial reporting.

What-if Statements
Pro Forma Accounting
Pro forma financials were once used strictly as an internal tool by management to review what-if scenarios such as how earnings would be affected if the company got into or out of a business, or what effect a particular merger would have on financial statements. Today, companies are cranking out another set of figures for the public to see as well. These financials are created outside traditional accounting principles (which are still required when reporting to the SEC) and are confusing to investors.

Generally Accepted Accounting Principles (GAAP) have been hammered out over the years by accountants, corporations, and regulators. They attempt to provide a consistent and objective way to compare financial results between companies. The objective of GAAP is to provide a fair and true picture of a company's financial position. It's debatable whether or not this objective is being accomplished, but the use of GAAP makes it somewhat challenging for management to hype their results to investors.

Some executives don't like to be restrained by accounting conventions. In pro forma accounting a company can present financial statements any way it desires. Management can use this as a tool to cast a more positive light on results. This is accomplished by conveniently ignoring selected expense items. Yahoo!, Inc. was one of the first to publicly emphasize pro forma figures. In January 1999 it presented results 35 percent better than GAAP by excluding a variety of costs related to buying other Internet companies. In 2000, Yahoo again released pro forma earnings that excluded additional expense categories.

An early version of pro forma reporting called EBITDA—earnings before interest, taxes, depreciation, and amortization—has become a popular number to report in earnings press releases. In a January 24, 2001, press release, telecommunications giant Qwest Communications reported $2 billion of EBITDA. Shareholders had to wait weeks for the GAAP reporting, which was found in a footnote to the annual results that showed Qwest actually lost $116 million.

The spread of pro forma earnings has plunged investors into an Alice-in-Wonderland world. In an article in *Business Week* in 2001 SEC chief accountant Lynn Turner called pro forma results "EBS earnings"—for Everything but Bad Stuff. "Way too often they seem to be used to distract investors from the actual results," Turner said.[5]

Pretend Sales

Vendor Financing

When a company lends customers money to purchase its products it's called vendor financing. In moderation this can be a sound marketing technique. But the potential for abuse in this area is pretty obvious. Essentially, sales can be fabricated. In the short run the lending company books sales and profits.

In the long run the company may be left with a questionable receivable. The financial worthiness of the customer-borrower may not be disclosed to investors at all or, if it is, the information is usually buried in the footnotes. If the customer doesn't make good on the loan, the house of cards collapses and ultimately hurts—you guessed it—the shareholders!

According to the *Business Week* article cited earlier, at the end of 2000, telecom-equipment suppliers were collectively owed as much as $15 billion by customers, a 25 percent increase from the year before. Effectively, they were buying their own products with their own money and as a result drastically exaggerating the size and sustainability of their sales and earnings growth.

A story on sales fabrication wouldn't be complete without the following report: On February 3, 2000, Motorola issued a press release announcing a $1.5 billion order from Telsim, Turkey's number-two wireless carrier. It wasn't until March 30, 2001, that investors found buried deep in a filing to the SEC that Motorola was owed $1.7 billion by Telsim. The fact that Motorola apparently lent Telsim 100 percent of the money to buy its products wasn't mentioned in the press release a year earlier.[6] On the day of the release the stock jumped by 5 percent to a split-adjusted $50 per share. It would have been useful for investors to be aware of this important fact at the time of the release.

It didn't take long for this loan to go bad. In April 2001 Telsim missed a $728 million installment to Motorola. The Uzan family, which controls Telsim, was charged in a 2002 lawsuit by Motorola and Nokia alleging that they fleeced the two telecom giants "through an elaborate scheme of deceit and intimidation" out of $2.7 billion of cash and equipment. If these companies had bothered to do a simple credit check, they would have found that the Uzans have a contentious history. In Turkish courts they are involved in more than 100 criminal and civil cases, with allegations ranging from money laundering to libel.[7]

A little over two and one half years after the initial press release announcing the "great news," Motorola stock was at $8, a drop of 85 percent.

Consumer Rebates: The Real Motive behind Them

Have you noticed the increased number of consumer products that have mail-in rebates? I have seen rebate programs that essentially make the product free to the customer. The company usually makes it a hassle to actually get the rebate and then counts on the fact that not everyone will apply for it.

The use of rebates and how they are accounted for gives companies yet another tool for the short-term manipulation of earnings. By using the rebate as a promotional tool a company can advertise a much lower price for its product relative to the competition. Of course, the lower price will have an asterisk next to it with the words "after rebate." The resulting increased sales for the period may make for a great press release and provide the desired temporary boost in the stock price.

However, the rebate is really a liability of the company that is incurred when the sale is made. Some organizations make a good-faith estimate of the percentage of customers that will actually apply for the rebate. Many simply overstate sales while ignoring the liability. Still others play with the estimate of how many will apply and show the rebates as advertising and promotion expenses instead of a reduction of sales. Investors like to see increasing sales, so the use of a rebate program is a way to artificially stimulate sales growth.

Hidden Liabilities

The Hypocrisy of Pension Reporting

"What's good for General Motors is good for the country and what's good for the country is good for GM," stated Charles Wilson, former chairman of General Motors, at his senate confirmation hearing as secretary of defense in 1953. Three years earlier Wilson was credited with launching the first modern pension fund. During the industrial boom of the 1950s, corporations flush with cash but short on workers offered defined-benefit pension plans to their employees. Within a year of GM's introduction, 8,000 similar plans were set up in America.

These plans guaranteed a specific monthly payment to employees at retirement. The companies put up all the money and invested a good chunk of it in the stock market to cover their future pension liabilities. Wilson felt that stocks were an ideal investment for the pension fund. Employees would have a direct interest in corporate profits and economic growth. In addition, such collective ownership, in theory, would soften people's attitudes toward big business.

Today, in lieu of the paternalistic approach, many companies opt for cheaper alternatives such as 401(K) plans in which the employees put up the cash and take on the investment risk. Even though defined-benefit plans may be considered dusty remnants of a bygone era, the fact is that these plans are still material to many U.S. companies. Over 70 percent of companies that make up the S&P 500 offer defined-benefit plans, or are obligated to pay retirees from previous plans, according to a study conducted by Credit Suisse First Boston (CSFB). These plans have been great for rewarding dedicated employees but have become an albatross for corporations struggling to meet their pension obligations.

In addition to setting aside funds for pension liabilities, corporations are required by federal law to pay premiums to the Pension Benefit Guaranty Corporation (PBGC), the government agency that steps in to provide some of the promised benefits of bankrupt companies. So pensioners are likely to receive most of their money, even though the PBGA recently announced a record $3.6 billion shortfall as of year end 2002, resulting from corporate bankruptcies that included Bethlehem Steel and National Steel. It's the shareholders who really stand to lose, followed by the federal government and its taxpayers.

Consider this: businesses are required by law to set aside money for pensioners. During the market boom of the 1990s companies juiced earnings from investment gains as the plans were overfunded from the stock market boom. As a matter of fact, according to the *New York Times,* an astounding 12 percent of the earnings growth registered by S&P 500 companies in 2000 came from pension income. IBM and General Electric are two companies that have used pension adjustments to help manage earnings, according to *Business Week.*[8] At year end 2002 it is estimated that pension plans in America owed $1.2 trillion to their current and future retirees, but because of the devastating carnage of an unrelenting bear market, there was only $892 billion set aside to foot the bill.

As if this isn't bad enough news, a peculiar quirk in accounting rules allows companies to estimate their pension fund investment returns over time and report the guess as profit, regardless of what actually occurs. Management has been able to legally distort the numbers to pad reported earnings—the bottom line that helps to determine top executive bonuses. In 2001, it is estimated that fifty of America's largest companies counted $54.4 billion of pension fund gains as profits, when in fact they lost $35.8 billion. If this kind of phantom accounting were used for other aspects of the companies' operations, the accountants would be doing jail time.

Financial Accounting Standard 87 (FAS 87) is credited with legalizing fictional pension accounting. Under intense lobbying from corporate interests, accountants who drafted the rule were convinced that including actual returns on pension assets would subject company earnings to increased volatility, which stock market investors don't like. As a result, companies can spread gains and losses over as long as five years. In addition, pension assets and liabilities are not listed on the balance sheet as such but rather as a "stub" amount that nets the two in the shareholder equity section. Pension accounting is a huge fiasco and brings back sour memories of Enron's numerous off balance sheet manipulations.

Let's look at General Motors, which now has more than two retirees to every employee on company pension and health care plans. In 1999, GM's pension plan enjoyed a healthy surplus with assets exceeding reported liabilities by 40 percent. Three years later the surplus turned into a colossal deficit. In early January 2003 GM announced that its pension assets were underfunded by $19.3 billion at the end of 2002, a $10.2 billion dollar increase from 2001. The GM plan has about $60 billion in pension assets compared to about $80 billion in reported liabilities.If we used commonsense accounting, GM should have reported an expense of at least $9.1 billion from the increase in its pension deficit. But common sense doesn't apply these days. GM showed a pension expense of only $1 billion and an overall profit of $1.7 billion for 2002.

GM announced that its expected pension expense for 2003 would triple to $3 billion and that its expected return on pension assets would fall from 10 percent to 9 percent. The average company uses a rate of 9.2 percent, according to the CSFB report. In 2002 GM's actual return on pension assets was a negative 7 percent.

The method used to calculate pension liabilities is an outrageous hypocrisy of corporate financial reporting that should be of even greater alarm to investors than the misreporting of pension expenses. The liability is a function of complex estimates of future pension payments based on factors such as the life expectancy of retirees and an estimated interest rate assumption. According to a study entitled "Pension Assumptions and Funding Levels: What Is Reasonable," corporate pensions are even more underfunded than actually reported. The analysis, completed by Stephen Church, president of Piscataqua Research Inc. in Portsmouth, New Hampshire, and William Strauss, principal of FutureMetrics L.L.C. in Bethel, Maine, concludes that companies use a high interest rate assumption to calculate pension liabilities, and as a result the amounts are severely understated.

A small change in the assumed interest rate can lead to huge changes in the reported pension liability. For example, in 2001 GM used a 7.3 percent interest assumption, similar to the median of 7.2 percent for all of the companies included in the study. The interest rate recommended by the Pension Benefit Guaranty Corporation in 2001 was 5.8 percent. At 7.3 percent, an $80 billion liability was estimated. If the recommended rate of 5.8 percent was utilized, the liability would balloon to approximately $100 billion, more than doubling the latest reported underfunding to $40 billion. Coauthor of the study Steve Church states that corporations "have used the full range of flexibility allowed in accounting rules to justify seemingly unreasonable assumptions."

And what effect would another $20 billion in underfunding have on GM's balance sheet? It would wipe out its entire shareholders' equity. GM would have more liabilities than assets. GM and other major companies are counting on the stock market to bail them out of this mess. It can be argued that the movement of the stock market is even more important to GM than the relative performance of its core automobile business!

According to *Employee Benefits Journal*, the average pension fund has upped its allocation to stocks from 40 percent in 1990 to 61 percent in 2001. Corporate pensions now find themselves the target of unflattering comparisons to the old S&L industry. Both attempted to boost income by purchasing assets with a much higher expected return but with little correlation to their liabilities. Both were legally acting as fiduciaries but treated their fiduciary role as a source of profit. Both are accountable to a federal insurer for any shortfalls, making their management decisions of public concern and consequence. Both have responded to unfavorable market performance by reaching for riskier assets with higher expected returns. Both have used accounting rules to paint the desired picture and conceal their errors.

PUBLIC RELATIONS FOR INVESTORS

We've now seen just a sampling of tools at corporate management's disposal if they desire to manipulate earnings, but this is only part of the equation in determining the price of a stock. Investor expectations are important in determining how the market will "capitalize" these earnings. Higher expectations mean a better P/E ratio and as a result a higher stock price. It's rare to see a company admit that its long-term future for success is not so bright.

The Big Bath

It may sound crazy that a company's managers would exaggerate losses, but sometimes they decide to write off as much as possible in a quarter or year when the numbers aren't good anyway. Of course the loss is downplayed and reported as an extraordinary (separate) item on the income statement. In essence the news release says something like "This write-off relates to past events and is not significant. It's now behind us, and we can focus on the future." These write-offs result from closing a division, the elimination of all the excess cost paid for an acquisition, or even the write-down of inventory. Anything that is listed as an asset on an organization's balance sheet can be written off if it is no longer considered of value.

When a company takes a "big bath," this means that assets are charged off as a one-time expense instead of being spread out over time. Therefore, future earnings will look relatively better because expenses will be reduced. It all comes down to creating the desired effect on the stock price. Believe it or not, the stock prices of some companies have rallied on the day of a press release announcing a big write-off.

Positive Spins on Negative News

On September 10, 2001, video renter Blockbuster Inc. issued a press release. The company stated that it would reduce its inventory on videocassette tapes by 25 percent and take a $450 million charge as a result. John Antioco, chairman and chief executive officer, stressed that it was a noncash charge and would result in no capital outlay. "The amount accounts for less than 1 percent of annual revenue," according to Antioco.

"This is really all about creating room and accelerating exposure to the DVD market," Antioco said. "It's potentially the fastest growing consumer product that's ever been introduced. This year's coming of age for DVDs is a major role in Blockbuster's strategy."[9] Corporate executives are often guided by public relations firms that have a technique for making bad news sound positive. There is an art to it.

I did a little "back of the envelope" accounting and came up with some interesting items that were not addressed in the Blockbuster press release. At the time of the release, the latest quarterly financial statements filed with the SEC, called the 10Q, were as of June 30, 2001. These are available to the general public on the SEC's web site through a system called EDGAR (Electronic Data Gathering, Analysis, and Retrieval). After my own analysis here are some notes and observations:

1. According to the Balance Sheet dated June 30, 2001, Blockbuster had an accumulated comprehensive loss of $88 million. That's a lot of money lost! With this announced write-off of the video inventory, I added another $450 million to the total losses. In other words, the company had lost $538 million of shareholders' money from the sale and rental of videos and games since its inception. Not very impressive.

2. For the six months ended June 30, 2001, the company had a loss of $10.9 million. They were continuing to lose money even before the write-off.

3. The rental library was shown as an asset on the books for $609.8 million. A write-down of $450 million represents almost 75 percent of the reported value from just

seventy days earlier. Yes, it may be less than 1 percent of sales, but this looks like a major event in my book. It was certainly downplayed as such by management.

4. As of June 30, 2001, the company had $8.1 billion in reported assets, $5.7 billion of which were intangibles such as goodwill. An intangible is usually worth nothing. It can't be converted to cash. More than half of this company's assets were *worthless!*

5. The company reported shareholders equity (assets minus liabilities) of $5.98 billion on June 30, 2001. At first glance this sounds like a company of substance. But wait a minute, what about that $5.7 billion of intangible assets? If you take that away, it leaves roughly $300 million of tangible shareholder equity as of June 30, 2001. Well, at least it's a positive number.

6. If the accounting was done properly, the $450 million write-off should have been matched against income during the years these items were being rented. Shareholder equity as of June 30, 2001 needed to be adjusted down by approximately this amount. After that adjustment I came up with negative tangible shareholder equity of $150 million. This means that liabilities exceeded tangible assets by $150 million. I decided to give the company the benefit of the doubt relating to the actual value of the remaining tangible assets on June 30, 2001.

7. I went back to Blockbuster's last press release relating to earnings to see if there were any clues about the upcoming write-off and the bad news about being, well, financially challenged. On July 24, 2001, the press release was extensive with lots of bold print: **Blockbuster Reports Strong Cash Earnings and Free Cash Flow for the Second Quarter of *2001*—EBITDA**

Increased to $118.4 million, on higher revenues of $1.23 Billion—Free Cash Flow Doubled to $75.2 million for the quarter; $175.1 million for the First 6 Months of 2001, Exceeding the Full Year Total for 2000.[10] The press release was a total of nineteen paragraphs that reiterated all the good stuff. It never mentioned that on a GAAP basis the company lost $15.6 million for the quarter. That was found by sifting through the financial statements.

8. I always find it interesting when companies emphasize that a write-off is a noncash expense. The write-off on the Blockbuster video library was technically noncash, but only because the cash used to pay for the videos had already been paid by Blockbuster in previous accounting periods.

9. My last observation has to do with the stock price and resulting market capitalization of Blockbuster. The market capitalization of a company is the result of multiplying the outstanding number of shares of a company by its current market price. As of the date of making these observations, the market cap for Blockbuster was $3.6 billion. This means that the market was stating that Blockbuster was worth $3.6 billion, even though it had a tangible net worth of a negative $150 million.

I don't want to pick on Blockbuster. It just happened to report a big bath and handled the PR like most other companies while I was working on this section of the book. However, just because Blockbuster is in the entertainment industry doesn't mean it has an exclusive on using fantasy and imagination to report and interpret corporate results. Sorry to say, their story is not unique.

NEW ISSUES OF COMMON STOCK

When a company issues common stock to the general public for the first time, it's called an initial public offering (IPO). During the late 1990s the hunger for new technology stocks by investors became seemingly insatiable. In some cases, with nothing to show but a business plan, a company could raise millions of dollars from willing investors. This was an extraordinary period in financial history rivaled only by other historic bubbles such as the Dutch tulip craze. The one thing that IPOs have in common, regardless of whether the stock goes up or down in the aftermarket, is dilution.

We've already seen how an investor's ownership in a company can become reduced or diluted by employee stock option plans. In an IPO the investor's share becomes immediately diluted because the price for a share of stock is greater than the book value per share of the company 100 percent of the time. The Internet entrepreneurs of the late 1990s who became instant millionaires didn't get that way by running profitable businesses. Their wealth was stolen from the multitudes of investors who were willing to suffer major dilution to own a part of their companies.

For example, ZZ Programmer establishes a company and puts together a business plan. He takes this plan to Wall Street, and the investment bankers like the idea and say it's marketable. ZZ sells 25 percent of his company to investors via an IPO for $10 million. This implies that 100 percent of the company is worth $40 million. ZZ just increased his net worth from zero to $30 million. Instant multimillionaire! On paper anyway. Of course this all came from the investors, who suffered immediate dilution. Since the company only has $10 million, less underwriting fees and commissions, and the new shareholders own 25 percent, the book value of their shares is $2.5 million, an immediate drop of 75 percent.

Of course companies don't always trade at a discount to book value. Some companies have traded at huge multiples of book value, even without current earnings. Why? It's fueled by investor expectations. During the "bubble" years of the late 1990s, huge multiples of book value were seen, as many investors seemed to lose touch with reality.

Confronting the Problem

In the past when executives went beyond the legal loopholes and committed fraud, we found that white-collar villains were in a class by themselves. The average jail sentence for corporate criminals in the S&L scandal of the 1980s was three years—twenty-nine months less than someone convicted for a first drug offense. And what about the three leading avatars of corporate greed during the 1980s—Michael Milken, Ivan Boesky, and Charles Keating? Keating spent less than five years in prison. Boesky spent two years behind bars and paid $100 million. Milken was sprung in less than two years, though he paid more than $1 billion in fines and settlements. But that's not to say he is feeling a financial squeeze. In 2002, Milken was reportedly worth a cool $800 million.

Boesky won $20 million, a house worth $2 million, and $200,000 a year for life in a divorce settlement. Keating is "tanned and fit" and "cutting a social swath" in Phoenix.[11]

■ ■ ■

In a baby step toward improving corporate governance, the Sarbanes-Oxley Act of 2002 requires the chief executive and chief financial officer to swear in front of a notary that "to the best of my (their) knowledge there is no untrue statement or omission of any material fact" within the financial statements. This should get management wondering whether the rewards for fraudulent accounting are outweighed by the prospect of a severe jail sentence. By providing a paper trail of evidence to the contrary, at least this takes away the defense that the chief executive had "absolutely no idea" that the company's financial officers were manipulating the figures.

The act quadrupled the maximum prison term for common types of fraud from five to twenty years. According to President Bush, this law was designed to "expose and punish dishonest corporate leaders." The sad thing about all of this is that the accounting for the majority of corporations is within the letter of the law. High-profile frauds such as what took place at Enron get plenty of press and attention, but the bigger underlying problem—lax accounting standards that give management too much leeway in financial reporting—goes on.

The proper accounting for pensions and stock options continues to be debated as companies use inconsistent methods to report on these items. According to Warren Buffett, the aggregate misrepresentation in just these two areas dwarfs the lies of Enron and Worldcom.[12] Today, some companies have opted to expense stock options, while others continue to insist these are not expenses. Many firms take advantage of pension accounting rules that allow them to record projected gains even when the values of their pension assets fall, while others take a more conservative route. And this is all within the framework of generally accepted accounting principles.

■ ■ ■

If we can't have complete trust in the financial reporting of corporations, perhaps we can count on Wall Street analysts to interpret the data and give us advice to help choose the companies that would be good investments. Or can we?

CHAPTER FOUR

FAITH IN PROFESSIONAL ADVICE
CONFLICTS OF INTEREST

*Well, the broker made money and the firm made money—
and two out of three ain't bad.*

ANONYMOUS

EVALUATING THE CORPORATION

I T'S A DIFFICULT JOB, at best, to evaluate the merits of a corporation as a potential investment. Interpreting the accounting, understanding how the business operates, and factoring in a host of other issues, including current investor psychology, can make the task pretty intimidating for even the most seasoned professional. But the decision as to whether a stock should be bought, held, or sold is made easier for most employees of the brokerage and investment banking industry because as a group they think it's always a great time to jump in and buy.

Investment Analysts

Investment analysts are researchers whose responsibilities include reporting on a particular company, following that company, and making recommendations on whether to buy, hold, or sell stock. With the emergence of CNBC and other investment-related media, analysts are continually in demand for interviews and their "educated" comments and recommendations. Their comments and stock ratings have become like gospel for certain investors. A new report on a company by these media analysts can have a dramatic effect on the stock price. In other words, they are influential figures in the investment world.

The investment industry hires analysts to do research on specific industry sectors, such as automobiles, oil, and technology, along with specific companies that make up a particular sector. Analysts who years ago worked almost unnoticeably from public view are now often the firm's public face. Two such analysts, Mary Meeker, of Morgan Stanley Dean Witter, and Henry Blodget, her peer at Merrill Lynch, both became media stars in the late 1990s and achieved powerful, almost godlike, status with individual investors.

Conflicts of Interest

A huge problem has developed over the years with analysts. In the old days analysts put out what was perceived to be unbiased research to grateful individual investors. Investment firms generated most of their revenues from stock trading by these individual investors. The modern analyst helps the investment banking team with identifying potential business from sources such as initial public offerings, bond underwritings, merger and acquisition activity, and so forth, and promises—implicitly at least—to "support" a company once it has gone public by giving favorable research. Honest, independent stock research is difficult if not impossible to come by.[1]

Investment firms and their analysts all speak a different language when giving advice on a stock. Not surprisingly the bias is always on the buy side—so much so that research departments of Wall Street firms have been widely criticized for not giving correct or clear ratings for the stocks they cover. The ambiguity is intentional to avoid upsetting the firm's investment banking clients. So researchers might give a rating of hold or accumulate when it should really be sell. The bottom line is that the conflict of interest between the analyst and the final reader of the report (the retail/individual investor) is so great that ratings don't really mean anything anymore.

■ ■ ■

When the markets test the extremes of reality, as was the case during the dot-com craze, some of the inherent problems in the industry become painfully obvious. Lawyers have to pass the bar, doctors have to go to medical school, and stockbrokers have to pass an exam and have a license before practicing. But stock analysts, who can make or break a company's stock with their research, don't need any credentials to practice their craft. Some stock analysts have achieved the Chartered Financial Analyst (CFA) designation, the fruit of a grueling program that tests topics from portfolio analysis and accounting to ethical standards. The two prominent Internet analysts mentioned earlier, Meeker and Blodget, are not CFAs.

Mary Meeker was important in popularizing the notion that the Internet industry was a giant "land grab" in which companies had to sacrifice profits for rapid growth. She was a leader in using new metrics to assess Internet companies. As the Internet exploded, she and other analysts became more aggressive about using nonfinancial statistics, such as page views and "eyeballs" to value companies. At the same time, she became more flippant about valuation. In 1997 Meeker wrote, "We have one general response to the word 'valuation' these days: 'Bull Market' . . . we believe we have entered a new valuation zone."

For a while, clients of Morgan Stanley Dean Witter (Meeker's employer) who bought Internet stocks were making tons of money, even with the wild valuations. It seemed like all the Internet stocks she was covering were doubling or tripling. And whenever one of them hit a bump in the road, she was quick to reassure one and all that everything would turn out all right in the end.[2]

. . . AND THEN IT ALL FELL APART

NASDAQ collapsed, dot-coms imploded, and the valuation bubble burst. Throughout the carnage Meeker refused to downgrade the stocks she followed, even as they dropped 70 percent, 80 percent, and in some cases over 90 percent. Her critics complained that the nonstop optimism was due to the fact that most of the companies she followed used Morgan Stanley Dean Witter as their investment banking firm.

Hear No Risk, See No Risk, Speak No Risk

On May 14, 2001, *Fortune* magazine published an article entitled "Hear No Risk, See No Risk, Speak No Risk (How a Bunch of Wall Street Analysts Hyped a Company Called Winstar to Death)."[3] Winstar, a former ski apparel shop turned broadband network and service provider, convinced the world that it was a legitimate high-tech up-and-comer and was an exceedingly eager participant in a system that rewarded companies for keeping up appearances at any cost. And analysts and investors were too blinded by greed, too captivated by an alternate financial reality known as EBITDA, and too tangled up in conflicted interests to raise questions—much less look at the company's balance sheet.

The sheer size and head-snapping speed of its decline made this company stand apart from the hundreds of other high-tech misadventures. In March 2000 its common stock hit a high of $65, giving the company a market value of about $10 billion. A little more than a year later, on April 18, 2001, Winstar filed for bankruptcy.

An analyst for Credit Suisse First Boston (CSFB), Mark Kastan, maintained his target price of $79 and continued to hype the stock, even as it dropped below $1 per share, until twelve days before the bankruptcy filing. In March 2000 CSFB and Salomon Smith Barney underwrote a $1.6 billion bond offering for Winstar and earned what one observer calls "really exorbitant" fees—more than $50 million.

In June 2000, Winstar management announced that they were "fully funded" through 2001. This assertion was repeated by analysts like Credit Lyonnais' Rick Grubbs, who initiated coverage on the stock on June 23, 2000, when the stock was at $40 with an $86 price target. All the while Winstar was employing all kinds of accounting tricks that should have been caught by at least one analyst.

On December 15, 2000, the company announced that it was fully funded through 2002, aided by a private placement of preferred stock to companies such as Microsoft and Compaq. In addition, Cisco and Compaq agreed to lend Winstar money to buy equipment from them. The sordid details of these kinds of wheelings and dealings (vendor financing) between companies are nauseating.

In February 2001 the company announced earnings for the year 2000. They were absolutely dismal, with bottom-line losses of over $1 billion for the year. Analysts were able to find a positive in the report since EBITDA losses had fallen to $153.4 million from $297.3 million the year before. "Better than expectations," raved Salomon Smith Barney's Jack Grubman, who called the stock "severely undervalued" and reiterated his $50 price target. Around this time the stock was selling for $11 per share.

In early March 2001 the outspoken short-seller Manuel Asensio released a series of devastating reports indicating that Winstar common stockholders had a high probability of losing their entire investment in a short period of time. He dismissed analysts as "idiots."

Salomon's Grubman characterized Asensio's report as "incomplete, inaccurate and inconsistent with our analysis." On March 13, CSFB's Kastan emerged from a meeting with Winstar's management and said that concerns about the company were overdone. He reiterated his buy rating and $79 target price on the $7 stock.

On Monday, April 2, Winstar announced that its required filing of financials with the SEC would be delayed. The next day, with Winstar now trading below $1, Glenn Waldorf, a new analyst at UBS Warburg, changed the rating to hold. Late on April 17 Winstar announced that it couldn't make its $75 million interest payment. With the stock at 14 cents, Grubman finally downgraded the stock to underperform on the day before the bankruptcy filing. Kastan simply dropped coverage of the stock.

Top Internet analysts like Mary Meeker and Henry Blodget made $15 million to $25 million per year (with bonuses) while exhibiting blatant disregard for the welfare of the firm's investing clients.[4] But the cash for those Wall Street bonuses came from investment banking fees, and the companies that generated those fees wanted praise, not criticism.[5]

■ ■ ■

Many a scorned investor pursued legal action against the brokerage firms. Of course, winning a lawsuit doesn't necessarily mean winning the fight. Attorneys are eager to take on such cases because of the huge potential settlement and contingency fees that range between 30 percent and 50 percent. As with most class action settlements, individual investors would see very little recovery of their losses, but the attorneys have the potential to reap huge windfalls.

In one of the biggest class action lawsuits of its kind so far, plaintiffs alleged that six major brokerages required their analysts to issue positive recommendations on certain Internet stocks in order to get investment banking business for the firms, and never disclosed that fact to the public. Those recommendations, the suit charges, led to investors' losses on overhyped securities.[6]

When the state of New York fined Merrill Lynch, Wall Street's largest broker, $100 million in May 2002 for pushing stocks to the public that it was privately bashing, none of the money went to the investing public. Out of the $100 million settlement, $48 million went to New York State, and $50 million went to other states, while $2 million went to the North American Securities Administrators Association.[7]

Given that all this advice from the brokerage firms was "free," investors certainly got what they paid for.

Alan Abelson, an editor at *Barron's,* has brought humor and a razor wit to his columns for over forty years. He had this to say about the qualifications for being a Wall Street analyst: "You should be equipped with the kind of face that doesn't scare small children when you make your obligatory appearances on Tout TV. . . . Knowing the difference between a bond and stock is helpful but not essential. The only true requisite is that, in good times and bad, come rain or shine, whether the market's woefully depressed or really flying, you must be bullish. And that means all day, every day, including weekends, lest you lose the habit."[8]

The Perpetual Optimists—the JDS Uniphase Example

In early 1999 JDS FITEL, Inc., based in Ontario, Canada, and Uniphase Corp., in San Jose, California, merged to create a new company called JDS Uniphase. The company manufactures lasers, amplifiers, and filters that are accessories to fiber-optic networks.

I had never heard of this company until late 1999 when several people asked me if this was a good investment. The company reported that profits and sales were increasing, but the stock seemed overpriced to me, even taking into consideration that the analysts asserted the company was well positioned in a "hot" industry.

JDS Uniphase decided to report its financial results in U.S. dollars and initially was led by Kevin Kalkhoven from Uniphase, who was cochairman and chief executive officer, along with Jozef Straus from JDS FITEL, who was cochairman, president, and chief operating officer.

For the twelve months ended June 30, 2000, the company had sales of $1.43 billion. That's a big number! It's hard for most people to relate to it. In the following analysis I have brought the numbers down to a level that is easy to comprehend by knocking off four of the zeros. Here is how the company would shape up if it were a small business for the twelve months ended June 30, 2000:

SALES	$143,000
COST OF SALES	75,000
GROSS PROFIT	$ 68,000
RESEARCH AND DEVELOPMENT	11,300
SELLING, ADMINISTRATION, ETC.	17,300
PRO FORMA PROFIT	$ 39,400

Note: JDS Uniphase actually showed a loss because of the amortization of goodwill and other items such as acquired R&D. I chose to ignore these items to attempt to show the company in the best light possible.

The balance sheet has some huge numbers on it, but a good portion is goodwill, which isn't worth anything. Goodwill is just a "plug" figure that is needed when one company acquires another company and pays more than the net worth of the purchased company. The adjusted balance sheet numbers would look like this:

TOTAL ASSETS	$2,639,000
LESS: GOODWILL	$2,234,000
TANGIBLE ASSETS	$ 405,000
LIABILITIES	$ 161,000
TANGIBLE NET WORTH	$ 244,000[9]

Now just imagine that this is a small business with tangible assets that exceed liabilities by $244,000, and that it currently has the potential to make a profit of around $40,000. However, this business has a chance to grow quite nicely. Sales have the potential to double or even triple over the next few years. That means profits could get up over the $100,000 level if everything goes exactly right. How much would you be willing to pay for this company? Remember there are no guarantees.

On July 26, 2000, there were 845 million common shares of JDS Uniphase outstanding, and they were trading at $135.83 per share. This is equivalent to saying that the company was worth $114 billion!

Bringing these numbers down to earth and relating them to my example, the market value of the company would be $11.4 million. If you took a company with $143,000 in sales and $244,000 in net assets to a small business broker and told him that you wanted $11.4 million for it, you would probably generate a hearty laugh and be quickly shown the exit for wasting his time. "But wait," you would say, "it has such great potential." The business broker would say, "You have a lot to learn about business."

I wouldn't have put a (adjusted) value of more than $500,000 on this company. Based on my quick look, the company was trading for more than twenty times what I thought was reasonable.

Here is a quick rundown on the stock price history of JDS Uniphase from July 26, 2000, to August 1, 2002 (adjusted for stock splits):

DATE	PRICE PER SHARE
JULY 26, 2000	$135.9375
SEPTEMBER 29, 2000	94.6900
DECEMBER 29, 2000	41.6875
MARCH 1, 2001	29.2500
AUGUST 29, 2001	7.1400
AUGUST 1, 2002	2.2900

At $2.29 the company had a market capitalization of approximately $3.6 billion, or about $360,000 if you lop off the four zeros. Hey, the price had finally reached the sanity range.

In 1999 JDS Uniphase's common stock was on fire. It began the year at a split-adjusted $17.25 per share and closed the year at $161.31. Now that's some serious price appreciation! The increase made no sense to me, but my early background was as a cautious accountant, not a stock speculator.

In the beginning of 2000 the price of the stock kept going up until it reached an all-time high of $293.06 on March 6, 2000—an increase of 82 percent in just a little over two months since the end of 1999. The people who asked for my opinion about this company in the middle of 1999 weren't very happy with me. I was told many times that I was too conservative. Investors in JDS Uniphase experienced a gargantuan increase in value during this period up to March 6, 2000.

■ ■ ■

In January 2001 *Kiplinger's Personal Finance* published an article with the title "Earnings Are so Passé." The article says to "look at sales growth to predict which stocks will make money. Indeed, examining sales numbers might make you a better investor. Two recent surveys confirm that growing or accelerating sales may be better indicators of which stocks will go up than the old standby, earnings growth."

The article went on to state the following: "PaineWebber recommends fiber optics player JDS Uniphase, one of the S&P 500 stocks with the fastest growing revenues over the past 12 months. Edward Kerschner, chief global strategist for UBS Warburg & PaineWebber states that stocks are trading on revenue growth rather than earnings per share. One reason is a growing skepticism over the reliability of corporate earnings figures, which a savvy chief financial officer can sometimes manipulate. Beyond that, revenues are a good measure of a company's ability to sustain earnings growth when profit margins fall."[10]

One way JDS Uniphase increased sales was by an aggressive acquisition program. I think it would have been good to use the overvalued stock to buy undervalued or even fairly valued companies, even if they were in an unrelated industry. Instead, JDS Uniphase used its overvalued stock to buy other overvalued companies in the same industry.

Its largest acquisition was a $41.5 billion buyout of rival SDL, Inc., announced on July 10, 2000, that closed on February 13, 2001. SDL was an optical-parts maker with 1999 sales of $187 million and profits of $25 million. Assets were less than half a billion dollars on December 31, 1999. SDL had an eye-popping $23 billion market capitalization on July 7, 2000, just before the acquisition announcement. This means that JDS Uniphase paid $18.5 billion more than the already lofty market valuation for SDL.

An article in the July 24, 2000, issue of *Business Week* entitled "Is JDS Uniphase Bonkers?" questioned management's sanity but found that some analysts thought it was a good deal. According to Conrad Leifur of US Bancorp Piper Jaffray: "If you factor in the synergies from the merger and the momentum of both companies, you can justify the price and show a path to higher earnings in 2001."[11]

JDS was still digesting seventeen acquisitions it made over the previous five years before the SDL announcement. Its latest acquisition, which closed on July 5, 2000, was the $18 billion buy of another rival, E-Tek Dynamics.

On March 31, 2001, JDS Uniphase had goodwill of $58.4 billion on its books. Goodwill, which has no value, accounted for approximately 90 percent of assets. Now the company was faced with amortizing the goodwill for the next five years, a charge of over $11 billion per year. That's huge! The company was projected to have only $3.5 billion in revenue for all of 2001.

A slowdown in the fiber-optic telecommunications market in 2001 made it painfully obvious that these acquisitions were not a good deal. On July 27, 2001, JDS Uniphase announced a loss of $50.6 billion. Of this amount, $50.2 billion was from amortization of goodwill and an acceleration of this amortization. They took the big bath. The press release mentioned a $270 million charge for the write-down of excess inventory and $500 million for a "global realignment" program. The program included a reduction of 16,000 employees.

Macleans quoted JDS Uniphase: "These are not real losses but *paper losses.*"

Much of the wealth creation was through undisclosed accounting fictions. Now that they got into the wealth destruction phase, the losses were dismissed as accounting fictions.[12]

In May 2000 Kalkhoven resigned. According to *Business Week* he had total compensation of $106.9 million in 2000.[13] According to the publication *Canadian Business,* Jozef Straus, the remaining CEO and chairman, "treated JDS Uniphase shares like hot potatoes—the second he got them, usually through exercising options, he's on the phone to his broker screaming sell, sell, sell."[14] Filings with the Securities and Exchange Commission indicate that Straus had unloaded 1.6 million shares, realizing a value of $150 million on the exercise of stock options during the fiscal year ended June 30, 2001.

JDS Uniphase was tracked by a bevy of analysts. Listed here are the analyst firms, dates, ratings, and prices of the stock on the day the recommendation was issued after JDS Uniphase hit its all-time high on March 6, 2000. Analyst recommendations were worthless, and the following provides ample evidence of that fact.

Analysts' Initial Coverage
Recommendations on JDS Uniphase

Date of Recommendation	Firm	Recommendation	Stock Price
March 22, 2000	W. R. Hambrect	Buy	$130.87
March 28, 2000	First Union Securities	Strong Buy	$129.06
May 25, 2000	Alex Brown	Strong Buy	$ 79.00
June 2, 2000	ABN AMRO	Buy	$110.37
June 13, 2000	Raymond James	Strong Buy	$121.37

The referenced firms that changed their recommendations in the following thirteen months did so as follows:

Date of Recommendation	Firm	Recommendation	Stock Price
April 20, 2001	W. R. Hambrect	From Buy to Strong Buy	$ 28.53
July 27, 2001	W. R. Hambrect	From Strong Buy to Buy	$ 8.55
Feb. 16, 2001	First Union	From Strong Buy to Market Perform	$ 35.81
Dec. 26, 2000	Alex Brown	From Strong Buy to Buy	$ 41.88
March 7, 2001	ABN AMRO	From Buy to Add	$ 26.94
June 15, 2001	ABN AMRO	From Add to Hold	$ 12.44
April 24, 2001	Raymond James	From Strong Buy to Market Perform	$ 20.82

Note: All data on prices as well as analyst recommendations from finance.yahoo.com.

Here is what several analysts were saying about JDS
Uniphase in late 1999:

*Susan Streeter, an analyst with Sproutt Securities Ltd., rates
the company a buy and expects shares to hit $330 in 2000. She
credits management with grabbing hold of this burgeoning
market in optical network infrastructure through a steady
stream of acquisitions.*

*Doug MacKay, manager of Red Oak Tech Select Fund, rates
the company a buy. He says, "It's a market that's just explod-
ing now."*

*John Wilson, analyst with Dillon Read, rates it a buy. "We
are on the front end of the curve in terms of the deployment
of optical technology."*[5]

If you took any of these analysts and their firms at their
word and purchased stock in JDS Uniphase as recommended,
you would have lost as much as 98 percent of your investment
principal. I admit it's a difficult if not impossible job to predict
whether a company should be bought or sold. But this was
crazy! And JDS Uniphase was only one of hundreds of companies that suffered price collapses while analysts fiddled with
their hopelessly sky-high price targets and recommendations.
As the market crumbled and analysts stuck with the same old
tune, investors learned another expensive lesson in who not to
trust.

How "Independent" Is the Audit?

A company's managers hire independent auditors to examine
their books and records and issue an opinion as to the presen-
tation of the financials to shareholders, creditors, and other
interested parties. It's very tedious work, and it's cost prohibitive for the auditors to verify everything. So the auditors rely

on management and their system of internal accounting controls as part of the auditing process. The auditors make a determination as to "fraud risk." If it is overestimated, then unnecessarily high audit costs will be incurred. This could directly affect the bottom-line profits of the accounting firm.

If the auditors decide that the financial statements are not correct and corporate management refuses to change them, the auditors will issue a qualified opinion and risk losing their client to another accounting firm. Management can choose whatever accounting firm they want and can change at will. It's a peculiar relationship. The corporation is the customer of the auditing firm, and it pays for the "stamp of approval" in the form of an unqualified opinion of its financials. A CPA is supposed to maintain independence and objectivity while performing duties as an auditor. But how can CPAs be independent from their client/customer when it's the customer choosing the auditing firm and paying the fee?

Many CPA firms also provide services in addition to auditing, such as tax preparation and planning. So, when they lose a client, they may be losing more than just an auditing fee. And what about the effect on independence and objectivity of a long-term auditor-customer relationship?

These are serious issues. A few countries such as Israel, Italy, and Spain have adopted mandatory rotation policies as a solution to the independence concerns. Changing auditors every few years would ensure that different audit "experts" review a corporation's representations. Auditors would have greater incentive to resist management pressures on ambiguous issues. Some suggest the auditors be appointed by a government agency to further distance the auditing firm from the corporation.

In any event, a structural problem exists with the system of auditing as it is practiced in the United States today. There is an inherent conflict of interest between the auditing firm and its client, the corporation, which makes it difficult for anyone to have confidence in the numbers.

The Fallacy of Professional Management

Statistical evidence consistently shows that professional investment advisers can't beat the market. As a matter of fact, every time you add a layer of complexity (as well as fees), total investment returns are diminished. Why is complexity synonymous with an investment professional? Well, if you are paying a fee for professional advice, you want to feel like the adviser is using his or her expert knowledge and experience, along with state-of-the-art investment software, to provide you with superior returns.

Investment professionals are taught the importance of diversification right from the beginning in Investments 101. However, there is a bias toward equities and equity mutual funds. Again, that unquestioned holy mantra in the investment field is *In the long run the stock market will always go up.* Mutual fund companies print and distribute a history of the stock market indexes going back seemingly to the beginning of time indicating that despite the bumps in the road the market just keeps increasing. Some advisers and brokers frame this chart and hang it in their office to give clients (and themselves) the reassurance that history is on their side. The country's largest retail broker, Merrill Lynch, has even selected a bull as its corporate symbol that goes in tandem with the "We're bullish on America" slogan. This is their permanent identity. I'm positive that I'll never see Merrill change its symbol to a bear with a new catch phrase like "We think the market's going down for a while."

When the market dips, investment advisers are fond of stating to each other, "This is where we earn our fees." The theory is that if the market always goes up in the long run, an investor shouldn't panic and get out of the market when it dips and everything looks so bad. The adviser feels that by holding their clients' hands through such periods and regurgitating the holy mantra (let's adhere to the *long-term* plan, we're *long-term* investors, etc.) that they are fulfilling their duties as the trusted adviser.

Many investors rode the market up during the "roaring nineties" all the way to the top in early 2000 and rode it right back down. Lots of investors got in toward the tail end of what is now viewed as a speculative bubble and lost significant sums of real money, not just paper profits. Even though indexes such as the NASDAQ composite were down by 70 percent in just a year and a half, most advisers stuck to their guns throughout the drop, telling their clients to stay the course and not worry—in the long run, that is.

Investment advisers and money managers do not have a crystal ball to tell them what will happen in the future. They have no more indication than you or I. It's the belief in the past that gives investment pros the confidence that the best advice to give an equity investor is to hang in there and keep the faith.

Check Out Receipt

Downtown - Elkhart Public Library
574-522-5669
www.myepl.org

Friday, September 27, 2019 3:18:40 PM

Title: Blind faith : our misplaced trust in the
stock market--and smarter, safer ways to invest
Due: 10/18/2019

Title: Dodd-Frank Wall Street Reform and Consume
r Protection Act : law, explanation and analysis
Due: 10/18/2019

Total items: 2

CHAPTER FIVE

THE REAL WINNERS OF THE STOCK MARKET GAME

An infectious greed seemed to grip much of our business community. It is not that humans have become any more greedy than in generations past. It is that the avenues to express greed had grown so enormously.

ALAN GREENSPAN, TESTIMONY TO THE COMMITTEE
ON BANKING, HOUSING, AND URBAN AFFAIRS,
U.S. SENATE, WASHINGTON, D.C., JULY 16, 2002

THE EXECUTIVE BENEFICIARY

THE INVESTORS who put their hard-earned dollars into the market take on the majority of the risk but receive only the crumbs of a market advance. The real winners are the executives, the brokerage industry, and the corporations. The potential rewards are so great that the behavior of these beneficiaries of market advances can range from unethical transgressions to outright fraud.

Executive Stock Options—the Fox Guarding the Hen House

The primary argument in favor of large stock option grants to executives is that they give incentive to focus on earnings growth since management benefits if the stock price increases. If the stock price goes up, current stockholders should be happy to reward management for a job well done. There are some major flaws with this line of reasoning due to the inherent conflicts of interest and shortsightedness created by stock option compensation.

In most companies the chief executive officer (CEO) gets the greatest amount of option grants, usually followed by other officers in the pecking order of the corporate hierarchy.

During the 1990s CEO compensation skyrocketed. A combination of generous stock option grants and ever-increasing cash salaries and bonus structures caused CEO pay to increase by an average of 571 percent from 1990 to 2000. In contrast, corporate profits were up an average of 114 percent, while worker pay was up 37 percent.[1] In 1980 the average CEO made forty-two times the average blue-collar worker's pay. Twenty years later the spread was a staggering 531 to 1.[2]

The trend continued during the year 2000. According to the AFL-CIO, the average CEO of a major corporation received $20 million of compensation in 2000. This included a 22 percent increase in salary/bonus and 50 percent increase in stock option compensation. The increase in option compensation is surprising given that in 2000 the S&P 500 index was down 10 percent and the NASDAQ composite index was down by 39 percent. By way of comparison the typical hourly worker received a 3 percent increase in total compensation, while salaried employees received about 4 percent more during the same period.[3] The twenty highest-paid CEOs earned an average of $117.6 million in 2000.

Walt Disney's Michael Eisner was the trailblazer of excessive executive compensation. Eisner's first contract at Disney made him so rich that other CEOs were green with envy. In 1995 Eisner was the highest-paid CEO in the nation at $194 million. The top figure for all CEOs in previous years was $75 million. Eisner's total pay for the three years ended in 2000 was $699.1 million. This was during a period when Disney stock actually returned a negative 10 percent to its regular shareholders, and reported net income fell by more than half, from $1.9 billion to $920 million.

The "independent" directors on many corporate boards are nothing but shams—typically handpicked by the CEO and loyal to him or her, even while serving on executive compensation committees that ratify bloated executive pay packages. Eisner answered to a board of directors that included the principal of his kid's elementary school, actor Sidney Poitier, the architect who designed Eisner's Aspen home, and a university president whose school got a $1 million donation from Eisner.

Fortune magazine investigated the board compensation committees that set CEO pay. They found that the committees are generally controlled by the CEOs themselves.[4] In a speech soon after publication of this article, Laura Unger, the acting chair of the Securities and Exchange Commission said, "Directors have an obligation to the company and its shareholders, not the CEO. Kow-towing to management and blindly signing off on large compensation packages is not a proper discharge of a director's duties."[5]

▓ ▓ ▓

According to the AFL-CIO, almost two-thirds of CEO pay is in the form of stock options. They give examples of excessive overpayments to executives who showed poor performance. Some of these executives were eventually fired or were forced to resign. These cases were referred to as "Poster Children in Executive Excess.[6]

STOCK PERFORMANCE VS. EXECUTIVE PAY

COMPANY	YEARS	CEO	CUMULATIVE FIVE-YEAR PAY	STOCK PRICE VS. S&P 500
Bank of America	1996–2000	H. McCall	$96.6 million	−34%
Sprint	1996–2000	W. Esrey	$218.4 million	−34%
Conseco	1995–1999	S. Hilbert	$146.2 million	−50%

In 1999 Charles Wang, CEO of Computer Associates, was deemed the highest-paid CEO for that year at $507 million. For the three years ending 2000 his compensation came to $698.2 million. During the three-year period the company's regular shareholders saw their Computer Associates stock drop in value by 63 percent. *Business Week* quotes Computer Associates spokespersons as stating that Wang was worth every penny of his pay.[7]

One of the craziest aspects of executive stock options is how they are handled when a company's stock goes down. In the event that the options become worthless, the board can simply issue more options at a much lower price, even below the stock's battered-down market value. The logic is that the CEO and key employees need incentives to stay on board and turn things around.

■ ■ ■

Fortune magazine published its own list of poster children in executive excess in an article aptly entitled "You Bought, They Sold" in September 2002.[8] Most everyone had heard about the corporate criminals of the day, including executives at Enron, Global Crossing, Worldcom, Adelphia, Tyco, and so on. But what were executives at other companies doing? The not-so-secret dirty secret is that even as investors were losing 70 percent, 90 percent, or even all of their holdings, top officials of many companies that had sunk the lowest were getting immensely, extraordinarily, and obscenely wealthy. They got rich because they were able to take advantage of the bubble to cash in hundreds of millions of dollars' worth of stock—stock that was usually handed to them via risk-free options—at vastly inflated prices. When the bubble burst, their shareholders were left holding the bag.

Only the largest companies, with greater than $400 million in market value, that had stock price decreases of 75 percent or more from peak to trough met the criteria of *Fortune's* study.

The time period for the report was January 1999 to May 2002. This amounted to 1,035 corporations where executives and directors hauled in roughly $66 billion. Of that amount, a total haul of $23 billion went to 466 insiders at the twenty-five corporations where the executives cashed out the most—approximately $50 million per person!

At the top of the heap was Phil Anschutz, a director at Qwest Communications, who received over $1.5 billion. Other Qwest insiders cashed out to the tune of another $750 million, according to *Fortune.* Qwest was once a $50 stock. Three years after the CEOs cashed in, it was less than $5. It didn't help when Qwest announced that it had inflated its revenues over three years.

The two top people at Broadcom brought in over $800 million each from stock sales. Anyway, you get the idea. The tragedy of all of this is that these huge windfalls were being siphoned directly from investors to enrich people who were not deserving of these rewards.

How the Real Money Is Made in the Stock Market

The highest price paid for a single-family home in the United States was more than $40 million for the old Hilton estate in Bel Air, California. The purchaser of this house was Gary Winnick, the CEO of Global Crossing, which now has the unenviable distinction of being one of largest companies to declare bankruptcy. In early 1999 the company was valued at $47 billion. Today it's close to zero. Consider that Winnick, a former associate of junk bond king Michael Milken, made over $700 million in profits from selling stock in this company that was driven into the ground on his watch.

According to *Business Week,* Winnick worked as a bond trader and salesman for thirteen years. Like most successful salesmen, his spending was partly for show. He carried cigars but rarely smoked them. His long-winded profanity-laced conversations tended to include a fair amount of name-dropping.[9]

Consider how the *real* money is made in the stock market. Look at Global Crossing. It went public in August 1998 and made instant millionaires of hundreds of insiders. As the company was hyped by Wall Street and increased in value, the insiders sold. People who ended up buying stock in the company as a long-term investment lost and lost big. In January 2002 the company went bankrupt. Just remember who lives in the most expensive single-family home in the United States and where that money came from.

■ ■ ■

Executive compensation packages have obviously gotten out of control and are a major problem. The packages create short-sightedness and a structural inducement to deemphasize long-term planning. Management is encouraged to focus on the short-term price movements of the company stock. Of course, this is usually not in the best long-term interest of the corporation or the shareholders. In addition, when the executives' own compensation is at stake, many become tempted to manipulate earnings and use other tactics in a desperate effort to prop up the stock price over the short run.

Executives of large corporations typically receive a cash salary in one year that would take the average employee several lifetimes of work to achieve. In addition, corporate executives pay nothing for the stock options granted by the board, which may or may not be offered to the lower employees. If the price of the stock goes down, the executive will still receive his or her salary, maybe a bonus, and other perks, such as the use of a company jet. But when the stock goes up, the executive stands to reap a windfall of wealth that dwarfs the cash salary. It's an unbelievably great deal for the executive. There are massive possible rewards without any risk at all.

Options dilute the value of stock held by investors for the benefit of the executive and other corporate employees. The bottom line is that it's a great deal for the executive and a raw deal for the investor. Excess option compensation is destructive to the continuing well-being of investors and can be a key factor in the destruction of the long-term health of the corporation.

Corporate Cancer

A serious disease afflicts the corporation, and it is causing a startling mutation in the very purpose of its existence. Traditionally, the corporation produces its product and sells its services with the intention of making a profit for its owners. The owner-shareholders elect a board of directors, which appoints management to run the affairs of the corporation for the owners' benefit. The owner-shareholders are willing to risk their capital in return for a reasonable return on their investment.

In the mutated corporation the board of directors and senior management appropriate funds from the owner-shareholders and focus their attention on the short-term movements in the stock price at the expense of long-term planning and sustainability. The transfer of wealth is now from the shareholders to management. The large corporation is being utilized as a mechanism for reassigning wealth from the general populace to a select few individuals.

No Relief for the Little Guy

Stockholders can't depend on the courts to protect their interests either, even when common sense would argue otherwise.

In October 1995 Michael Ovitz was hired to be president of the Disney Corporation. His employment was rocky from the start, and less than one year later he was seeking employment elsewhere. Ovitz and the board of Disney agreed to a severance payment valued at $140 million.

Shareholders sued the board alleging that Ovitz should have been fired for cause and that his termination was at the very least a voluntary resignation. The Delaware Supreme Court agreed with the lower courts and said that the board acted with sound business judgment in that the exchange was not so one-sided that no businessperson of ordinary intelligence could conclude that the company did not receive adequate services for the money involved.[10]

Because of favorable accounting treatment, tax incentives, and court rulings of this nature, it is likely that the use of stock options will remain an essential element of the executive compensation plan. Disgruntled shareholders seeking to curb the excess through the courts are fighting an uphill battle. The courts encourage shareholders not to depend on the legal system for relief.

THE CORPORATE BENEFICIARY
Using Stock As Currency

It seems that hardly a day goes by without news in the financial press about a new merger or acquisition of one company by another. When one company purchases another it is financed either by cash, stock, debt, or a combination of all three. We've already seen how corporations use their stock as a substitute for cash to compensate top management. Another creative use of company stock is for acquisitions of other companies.

In the 1960s there was a flurry of merger and acquisition activity in what could be called the "conglomerate boom." Antitrust laws kept large companies from purchasing firms in the same industry, so creative entrepreneurs went on to purchase businesses in completely different fields without any hassle from the Justice Department. The motivation behind these purchases was that the acquisition process itself could produce growth in earnings per share. With an easy bit of basic accounting magic, they could put together a group of diverse companies and produce rising earnings per share for a period of time.

The accounting trick that makes this game work occurs when a company that has a high price-to-earnings ratio swaps its high-multiple stock for the stock of another company with a lower multiple. For example, assume that Hi-Tech Growth Company earns $1 per share, has 1 million shares outstanding, and a P/E ratio of 50. This means the stock sells at $50 per share. Hi-Tech Growth decides to buy Old Tyme Meat Packing, a company that earns $1 per share, has 1 million shares outstanding, but sells at a P/E ratio of 10. This means Old Tyme stock sells at a price of $10 per share.

Hi-Tech rolls in and offers Old Tyme shareholders $15 per share, or 50 percent more than the current trading price, in the form of Hi-Tech stock. Therefore, Hi-Tech issues 300,000 ($15 million/$50) new shares to Old Tyme shareholders for 100 percent of the company. The next year, Hi-Tech and Old Tyme earn the same amount, $1 million each, for a total of $2 million. Hi-Tech shows an increase in earnings per share of almost 54 percent to $1.54 ($2 million/1.3 million), even though the earnings for both organizations were flat.

Investors see over 50 percent growth rates in earnings per share when in reality the conglomerate literally manufactured growth. The more acquisitions of this kind Hi-Tech can make, the faster earnings per share will grow, making the stock even more attractive to investors. This ploy makes top management look like geniuses when in reality it is just another accounting deception.

As a side note, in the 1980s many of the old conglomerates began to play the game of deconglomeration. In order to boost earnings, the old conglomerates began to shed their unrelated poor-performing acquisitions that were mismanaged and losing money.

■ ■ ■

The new-technology bubble of the late 1990s caused a lot of high-tech companies to have sky-high price to earnings multiples. Many of the companies couldn't be evaluated by this traditional ratio because they didn't even have positive earnings. Mergers and acquisitions came into vogue again as companies used their high-priced stock in exchange for other companies. However, in most cases there was a large contrast between the strategy of the conglomerates in the 1960s and that of high-technology companies in the late 1990s. The focus wasn't on immediate profit but on establishing a commanding lead in market share in an area that had the expectation of tremendous growth in the future. It became common for companies to issue hundreds of millions or even billions of dollars worth of stock for a company that had only a fraction of the acquisition price in tangible assets.

Many corporations that were graced with these colossal valuations just couldn't seem to help themselves from going after other companies. Lots of the deals had shareholders scratching their heads, but most bought into the concept that the potential future business was so huge that the premium prices being paid for these companies were justified. Besides, the accounting treatment on these acquisitions was very favorable to the acquirer.

When Goodwill Turns Bad

There used to be two accepted means of accounting for a merger. One was by the *pooling of interests* method. The other was by the *purchase acquisition* method.

According to a study completed by PriceWaterhouseCoopers, over 60 percent of the mergers valued at $500 million or more between 1994 and 1997 were accounted for using the pooling method. The method was very simple: you simply added the balance sheet items of the two companies together. If a company exchanged stock worth $5 billion for another with assets of only $1 billion, you simply ignored the extra $4 billion that was paid. Shareholders' stake was diluted, but this excess cost was never charged to earnings. Corporate executives loved it! Management could overpay for ego-gratifying acquisitions, and the cost of this stupidity never showed up anywhere. Pooling of interests was the dominant method used in the conglomeration boom described earlier. Pooling was completely idiotic, and the only reason it was accepted for so long was because of intense lobbying by business.

In the purchase acquisition method, any premium paid in excess of the acquired company's book value gets recorded as goodwill. This is amortized over time, which causes a decrease in earnings because of the amortization expense. Usually, the goodwill is written off over a period of about five years.

The SEC spent a lot of time on the merger accounting issue and wanted to set up standards to strictly limit and phase out the pooling method of accounting for acquisitions. A resounding majority of senior corporate executives wanted to keep the pooling method. It has become a political issue, with subcommittees of Congress hearing arguments from corporations and accounting firms. The bottom-line argument for utilizing the pooling method was that the alternative purchase acquisition method resulted in lower reported earnings per share.[11] If earnings per share decreased, the stock would likely decrease in price, and no one is going to be happy about that.

Even when companies were forced to use the purchase acquisition method, they tried to minimize the amortization impact on earnings by pointing out that this was a noncash expense. Some companies decided to take the big bath in one quarter and write off all the goodwill at once as a separate line item on the income statement. Again, they emphasized that this was a nonrecurring, noncash charge.

New accounting pronouncements require that companies use the purchase method instead of the pooling method when accounting for acquisitions, but now goodwill is treated as a *nonwasting* asset. This means that goodwill can stay on the books permanently unless impaired. And impairment is based upon the judgment of management and their auditors. Close one loophole and open another.

Too Little, Too Late

The regulators are backlogged with reviewing corporate financials. Aggressive or questionable accounting practices can slip through the cracks or take years to clamp down on. By the time regulators take action the company may be out of business or may have hoodwinked investors long enough to use its overpriced stock to issue additional securities for cash and/or acquisitions to feed its growth.

One such scenario of regulators catching up after the fact is America Online (AOL). For years AOL sent out millions of computer disks to potential customers to entice them to try its services. Personally, I must have received at least a dozen of these by direct mail. Like any other junk mail, I immediately disposed of these disks and wondered to myself how much the company was spending on this marketing program and whether everyone else around the country was getting multiple offers to sign up with AOL. It turns out AOL was spending a truckload of money on distributing these disks and aggressively deferring these expenses on their financial statements. This means that the bulk of this marketing expense was carried as an *asset* on the company's balance sheet. This accounting ruse allowed AOL to dramatically overstate its profits. Investors were totally enamored with an Internet company that was actually making a profit and mindlessly continued to buy the stock. It's almost certain that AOL stock would have been trading at a much lower level if its accounting had been done properly.

AOL made the most of its high-flying stock by making many aggressive acquisitions. For example, in November 1998 AOL agreed to acquire Netscape in a pooling of interest transaction valued at $4.2 billion. Netscape at the time had a book value of $394 million. Since the acquisition, the Netscape brand name has all but disappeared, and many of the company's talented people, including founder Marc Andreesen, left AOL. In other words, AOL probably spent about $3.8 billion too much. This loss never had to be reflected in the income statement because AOL used the pooling of interest method for the merger.

On January 10, 2000, AOL announced that it was acquiring communications giant Time Warner, a much larger organization in every respect. According to the press release:

> America Online, Inc. and Time Warner Inc. today announced a strategic *merger of equals* to create the world's first fully integrated media and communications company for the Internet Century in an all stock combination valued at $334 billion. To be named AOL Time Warner Inc. with combined revenues of over $30 billion, this unique new enterprise will be the premier global company delivering branded information, entertainment and communications services across rapidly converging media platforms.[12]

On May 15, 2000, after an investigation by the SEC turned up the improper accounting, AOL submitted to a settlement (without admitting or denying any wrongdoing), paid a $3.5 million fine, and restated its prior reported income to losses. Of course, by that time the company was home free. AOL had already used its overinflated stock to buy one of the largest news organizations in the world.

By the way, the $3.5 million fine paid by the company pales in comparison to the $349.7 million made by Steve Case, chairman and CEO of AOL from 1998 to 2000. The merger deal generated stock option bonanzas for Case, his deputy Robert Pittman, and Time Warner's top five executives, totaling an estimated $3 billion. Another interesting note is that in the three years after the initial merger announcement the market value of the combined organization has gone from $334 billion to approximately $60 billion.

THE INVESTMENT INDUSTRY
BENEFICIARY

When a company decides to do a direct offering of its stock to the public, there is no law that says it must go through a Wall Street investment bank. However, very few firms are able to do this on their own unless they are only attempting to raise a modest sum of money. The investment banking industry has the infrastructure to raise huge sums of cash for corporations with the support of a distribution system composed of brokers/advisers, research analysts, and valued contacts with institutional money (the *really* big money). Investment bankers serve as intermediaries between the corporations that need to issue stock or bonds and the investors willing to invest in such instruments.

I've already given examples in Chapter 3 of the significant dilution that occurs for the investor in an initial public offering (IPO). The conflict of interest that exists for the company that wants to get as much money as possible and give up as little of the company as feasible is readily apparent. This conflict and the significant dilution are readily disclosed in the IPO offering document. Now if only the investor had the inspiration and time to read as well as comprehend the report.

An institutional investor has access to large sums of money with the primary purpose of investing a large percentage of these funds in the securities markets. Investment bankers savor their relationships with these organizations. It's the institutions that provide funding for the bulk of IPOs as well as bond offerings.

When an IPO is brought to market by an investment banker, who is the actual client of the investment banker? Is it the corporation for whom the money is being raised? Or is it the retail investor who has a brokerage account with the firm? What about the institutional investor? The answer of course is that all are clients, but all are not treated equally.

Exorbitant Fees

In 1999 and 2000 companies raised approximately $121 billion from 779 IPOs. Of that amount, over $8 billion was paid to investment banks in the form of underwriting fees. However, that is only a fraction of the true cost to the companies issuing new stock. The investment banks priced the stock far below the full market price—measured as the price reached on the first day of trading. This cost amounted to $62 billion. In other words, for every dollar raised by the underwriters, corporate America paid 57 cents in fees and foregone proceeds.[13]

In lieu of selling the shares to those willing to pay the most, Wall Street handed the underpriced shares to a privileged group of institutions that frequently trade with the investment banks. This was a nice windfall to the institutions. They were able to purchase stock at the offering and benefit from the huge demand for IPOs by the retail investor, who was willing to pay dizzying amounts over and above the offering price. On the first day of public trading, prices jumped an average of 71 percent in 1999 and 57 percent in 2000. These kinds of numbers only occur in a hot market, and the investment banks certainly made hay while the sun shined.

The investment banks would have received higher underwriting fees if they had priced the IPOs correctly. But they received far higher income from trading revenues. In exchange for the low-priced shares that were practically guaranteed to jump once they started trading, institutions gave the investment banks huge commissions that reached an outrageous $1 per share. The SEC wonders whether these unusually high commissions were actually "kickbacks" to the Wall Street firms in exchange for the shares. Private lawsuits describe these commissions as "excessive and undisclosed."

According to Michael Tennenbaum, former vice chairman of investment banking at Bear Stearns, "Wall Street has always attracted greedy, power hungry people."[14] In the past, investment bankers had to sell offerings at about 10 percent below their estimated price once the stock started trading. The institutions clamored for this cheap stock. But in return, the firms asked that the institutions hold the stock for at least several months. In 1999 and 2000 the prices were up so much that the institutions sold immediately, a practice referred to as *flipping*, and used the proceeds to get in on another IPO. It worked out great for the institutions and the investment banks, but not so well for the individuals who bought in at the high.

"Spinning" Out of Control

Investment banks used the inexpensive stock as a perk to get business. They would often hand shares of a current IPO to the founders and majority owners of still privately owned corporations, guaranteeing them a nice fast profit—a practice called *spinning*. Wall Street needed a steady source of new IPOs to keep the money machine cranking. Essentially, this meant that Wall Street was using what should have been another issuer's money to pay for the firm's own marketing expenses. The investment bank had control over the distribution of the underpriced stock, and they used it to their advantage wherever and whenever possible.

Corporate America was a loser in that *they* should have received the benefit of their overpriced stock, not the institutions and their own investment bank. But the biggest loser, as always, was the individual retail investor. Individuals had no access to IPOs unless they were in a position to benefit the investment bank. They bought stock after the opening of trading and paid the huge premiums over the IPO price. By the size of the trades, you could tell that these were small investors, and it was their willingness to purchase that allowed the institutions to sell and make a quick buck.

Just six months after the 779 IPOs of 1999 and 2000, 75 percent of these firms traded at prices below the initial offering price. Two years later many of these companies were trading at a fraction of their offering price or had gone out of business.

The small investor who bought into these at the opening-trading price and is holding for the long term is now a *minuscule* investor.

STEERING CLEAR OF THE INSANITY

The common assumption that the best prescription for prosperity is a free market economy in which the government allows substantial freedom for businesses to pursue profits has been corrupted by the degenerative evolution of the corporation. Adam Smith, the late-eighteenth-century Scottish economist, addressed this issue in his magisterial work *The Wealth of Nations.* This writing has served, perhaps more than any other single work in the economic field, as a guide to the formulation of governmental economic policies.

Adam Smith believed that owners, not managers, exercise the greatest diligence in the efficient use of assets and capital.

> *The directors of such companies, however, being the managers rather of other peoples money than of their own, it cannot well be expected, that they should watch over it with the same anxious vigilance with which the partners in a private copartnery frequently watch over their own. . . . Negligence and profusion, therefore, must always prevail, more or less in the management of the affairs of such a company.*[15]

This was written in 1776, but its message is certainly timely. Adam Smith, deemed the father of capitalistic thought by many economists, believed that it was best for the individual to invest locally because of the inability to supervise his or her capital when it was far from home. He did not conceive of a corporate structure that disconnects the rights and powers of ownership from the consequences of their use. The fact is that the most shareholders can lose on a stock investment is the amount of their investment. Owners are shielded from any liability resulting from the consequences of management activities and are kept largely unaware of actions taken in their name for their exclusive benefit. They are given historical reports that, as we have seen, do not always portray the truth.

The Enron case provides a dramatic example of the outright corruption that is possible in our financial system that goes far beyond the "negligence and profusion" predicted by Adam Smith. Enron was led by arrogant executives with inflated egos, who refused to admit that they made grave errors in business judgment and hid their mistakes through creative accounting maneuvers. Wall Street, anxious to do business with the seventh largest company in the country, continued to recommend Enron. This enabled the stock price to remain artificially high as insiders cashed in their options and made hundreds of millions of dollars, all the while encouraging the rank-and-file employees not only to hold but also to buy more stock. Enron had paid Wall Street firms over $320 million over the years in underwriting and consulting fees. As late as September 26, 2001, Chairman Kenneth Lay urged employees to buy the company stock and assured them in an internal memo that "the third quarter is looking great." This was three weeks before the company announced a $638 million third-quarter loss as opposed to projected profits.

The only airtight solution for investors is to avoid gambling on the uncertain returns of individual stocks and mutual funds by developing a personal strategy for dealing with threats to the safety of their investment principal.

PART II

STRATEGIES FOR DEALING WITH UNCERTAINTY

REDEFINING RISK MANAGEMENT

Today we could with total truth be called a nation of speculators . . .
THE NEW MCCLURES, A POPULAR MAGAZINE OF THE 1920S

CONVENTIONALLY DEFINING RISK

ONE OF THE first steps to developing a financial plan involves taking an accurate assessment of what you own and owe, along with your sources of income. The next step is to get a handle on your attitudes toward risk and a clear understanding of your goals and objectives. This might be determined from a series of questions that you ask yourself or from an interview with a financial planner. The answers to these questions are important components in determining an appropriate investment plan because your risk tolerance level determines your overall approach to investing.

Investors define *risk* as the probability or likelihood of losing money. Here is a listing of risks that are traditionally of concern to investors:

Market risk—the probability of losing money in the securities markets

Interest-rate risk—the chance of being tied to a low rate for a long period of time when interest rates go up

Reinvestment risk—the investment of future cash flows at a reasonable rate of return

Credit risk—the chance of a company failing to meet its obligations

Common factor risk—nondiversification

Inflation risk—changes in the real value of money and investments

Holding period risk—the chance you have to sell too soon (or hold too long)

All of these risks are legitimate and should be considered when constructing an investment plan. Once it is determined whether you are a risk taker, a risk avoider, or somewhere in between, a specific plan can be constructed.

If you are working with a financial planner, a plan is eventually agreed upon, implemented, and on a periodic basis the portfolio's performance is reviewed and the investments rebalanced. Many financial advisers develop what is called an Investment Policy Statement (IPS), which summarizes the fundamental investment goals and objectives and how these goals will be achieved. The IPS states the asset allocation targets, boundaries, and diversification parameters in an attempt to match the limits of risk that the investor is willing to assume. It includes guidelines for determining specific asset classes and allows for excluding certain types of companies from the portfolio.

Diversification Reduces Risk, but Does Not Eliminate It

One of the most important parts of the plan will include some sort of "asset allocation," which is the process of identifying and selecting asset classes and determining the appropriate percentages for the portfolio (in other words, figuring out how the money is to be divided). By examining historical data, the planner (and trusty computer) can determine an optimal mix of asset classes, subclasses, and so on, that increase the probability of an investor achieving the agreed-upon goal at a certain risk tolerance.

The decision of how much goes into each category (stocks, bonds, or cash, for example) has proven to be even more significant than the selection of the specific stock, fund, real estate, or other investment and may account for as much as 80 percent of the overall return on the portfolio.

A study conducted by Brinson, Hood and Beebower in 1986 concluded that 93.6 percent of a portfolio's performance depends on asset allocation. The study concluded that the asset allocation decisions made by investors are by far the single greatest determinant for future investment success.[1] The money management industry has been preoccupied with the role played by asset allocation ever since this proposition. Brokerage firms continually update and publicize their calculation of the ideal asset allocation mix.

Historical data indicates that when one class is doing well, another may be decreasing or not increasing as much. The measure for this difference is called the *correlation coefficient*. If your portfolio consists of investments that are negatively correlated—meaning that if one is going down the other is going up—it gives you more diversification and consequently less risk. This is a great idea in theory, but history doesn't always repeat itself. For example, the stock market doesn't always go up when interest rates go down. International markets don't always go in the opposite direction of U.S. markets.

By using diversification to smooth out the ups and downs that occur in each asset class, risk is reduced. This process was invented in the early 1950s and was described in the book *Portfolio Selection* by Harry Markowitz.[2] University professors with scholarly statistical backgrounds expanded on the work done by Markowitz. Wall Street and investment professionals picked up these academic theories in the 1980s. Computers cranked out statistics, and trendy risk measurement jargon such as alpha, beta, and R Square were bantered about and began showing up in client reports.

The basic principle behind all the statistics remains the same—*diversification reduces risk*. The problem is that diversification does not *eliminate* risk. Diversification can reduce the risk of owning stock, but it can't reduce the risk associated with macroeconomic events that can threaten all businesses. This risk, referred to as *systematic* or *market risk* by the number crunchers on Wall Street, is essentially the risk associated with the overall market decreasing.

To summarize, traditional investment risk management is a simple process. First a long-term investment plan is created with asset allocation percentages that match your goals. Then the portfolio of investments is selected and is properly diversified to guard against the risk associated with having too much in any security. The focus is maintained on long-term goals. The basic assumption is that the markets have a history of short-term ups and downs but always go up over time.[3]

Market Timing or Random Luck?

Wall Street has always had a problem dealing with systematic risk. Hypothetically, investors could attempt to reduce this risk through market timing, which involves strategically determining when to buy and when to sell. As we know, timing is everything; hence the old adage "buy low, sell high." But how do we know when we have reached the lows and the highs? The answer is simple: we don't, and neither does anyone else. Timing the market, like beating the market over the long run, is the stuff of dreams. The overwhelming conclusion of research on this topic is that any success in market timing is based purely on random luck.

Since market timing doesn't work, advisers recommend a benchmark strategy of buying and holding. This passive strategy calls for purchasing an investment and leaving it alone for a long time. Periodically, you would "rebalance" your investments so that your asset allocation percentages remain in line with your investment plan.

Market risk is supposedly mitigated by our unfailing faith that stocks will do well over the long run. As a result, professionals expend a lot of brain cells on calculating *beta*—a portfolio's sensitivity to market risk. Beta is simply a measure of volatility. A portfolio with a relatively low beta means that if the overall market goes down, the portfolio will also go down in value but not as much as the market. So if the market is down 10 percent, a low beta portfolio may only be down 5 percent. This applies to rising markets as well. If the market is up 10 percent, the low beta portfolio may be up only 5 percent. A low beta portfolio may be termed conservative but could still go down in value if the market goes down.

Many investors (as well as advisers) focus on the beta. If you buy into the theory that the market always goes up, you'll focus on the risk of not doing as well as the market does, or missing out on upside gains. This is why many have opted to purchase index funds that go up and down in tandem with a particular market index. The risk of deviating from the market averages is virtually eliminated with an index fund. Indexing will be discussed in Chapter 8.

Computer Modeling

I agree that employing historical data to come up with an investment plan is useful, but it is overplayed by the investment community. The average person can be taken in by the impressive computer modeling accompanied by the array of graphs, pie charts, and statistical references supplied by investment advisers. I've concluded that most of this information isn't useful and is basically fluff to give clients the impression that they are dealing with a firm and/or person with superior intelligence. The complexity actually seems to increase investors' comfort level. But the projections do nothing to reduce market risk and are correct only insofar as the assumptions are accurate.

In the late 1940s, scientists at Los Alamos National Laboratory programmed their computers to create random combinations of known variables to simulate the range of possible nuclear-explosion results. They nicknamed the program Monte Carlo, after that city's famous roulette wheels, and used it to find patterns that would let them plot the probability of different outcomes.

Today, many financial planners use Monte Carlo–style simulation calculations to determine how long a certain amount of money invested in a certain way will last if drawn upon for retirement. Baseline information, such as age, current value, and composition of investments, is plugged into the program along with assumptions such as life expectancy, future inflation, and investment returns. The program spits out the amount of money you can comfortably withdraw each month with a certain level of probability.

This is a nice retirement planning curiosity, but that's about it. Investment return assumptions are usually based upon past history, which isn't necessarily going to repeat itself. The simulations can't accurately project how markets will behave in the future, and as a result the computer projections may give the retiree a false sense of security.

Inflation Risk

The possibility of losing the purchasing power of your capital is inflation risk. This is usually the primary justification for investing in the stock market. If the purchasing power of the dollar becomes less and less over time, we need to have some mechanism for staying ahead of the erosion. Real estate and other tangibles have proven to be good inflation hedges while having their own unique risks. Low-interest accounts, such as checking and interest bearing CDs, are usually a poor inflation hedge. A long-term commitment to the stock market has traditionally been considered a good inflation hedge. However, as stated earlier, an investment in the market subjects us to the most challenging puzzle of risk management—*market risk*.

It is forever essential to have a healthy respect for risk and its potential to destroy wealth. Uncertainty of the future is a constant issue. A man-made or natural disaster such as terrorist hostilities or a massive earthquake could occur without warning at any time. These types of events can have far-reaching economic consequences. Most people ignore these risks, taking comfort in the certain data of the past and believing that it is a reasonable forecast of the future. We have the unique ability to rationalize away the lessons of our past. This excerpt from an article published in the late 1920s could easily be compared to the overheated market of the late 1990s:

> *Today we could with total truth be called a nation of speculators. People are cautious with their goods and materials but at the same time there has been an unprecedented, unrestricted and unrestrained buying of stocks. America has experienced other booms—railway booms, real estate booms, the rubber boom, the Alaska boom, and, most recently, the Florida boom. But America has never known a boom so vast, so colossal, or involving so many billions of dollars as the Coolidge bull market.*

> *The media was fanned by endless newspaper stories of how this one and that one and the next one had transformed a few hundred or few thousand dollars into a fortune sufficient to yield luxury for the rest of the lucky one's life. As stock prices have rose and rose the speculative fever has been increasing in intensity. Almost every Tom, Dick and Harry—as well as Harriet—is convinced that a royal road to wealth has opened up. All sorts and conditions of people have been dabbling in stocks. Many boast of their intelligence in picking stocks. Others quietly accumulate stocks in this frenzied market.*[4]

As long as human emotions are a factor in financial decision making, we are likely to repeat the lessons of the past and experience periods of frenzied euphoria followed by times of despair and depression.

Acceptable Risk

I consider myself a conservative investor. I don't mind not making as much as the market when it's going up, but I definitely don't want to lose money. I would like to see my overall investment portfolio increase in value each year regardless of how the market performs. A 10 percent drop in value is unacceptable to me. It's irrelevant whether I lose less than the overall market. What if the market is down 40 percent? Is it supposed to make me feel good if I'm only down 20 percent? That doesn't make sense. I want protection against loss!

Even though the market may have been one of the best places to put money over the last sixty years, I am not going to put my blind faith in the consensus that it will be so in the future. Trust just doesn't cut it anymore. The betrayal of trust by corporations, brokerage firms, accountants, and regulators has taught me that much. I look at the future of market returns simply as a string of random numbers. Some years the numbers are positive. Some years the numbers are negative. And in some years they are basically unchanged. Of this I am certain.

Given what I know about the uncertainty of stock market investing and my nearly schizophrenic approach of wanting to avoid loss yet participate in gains, there is a risk management strategy that satisfies both my desire for safety and need for potential growth.

Mitigating Market Risk

Most of us would not think twice about whether or not to have insurance on our house. When an insurance company issues a policy they are concerned about things such as potential defective wiring and locks, flammable substances stored in the garage, and anything else that increases the chance of loss. These are called physical hazards. Insurance companies also have to guard against fraudulent claims and dishonesty. This increases the chance of loss, and this is called a moral hazard. Insurance will cover specific causes of loss, such as fire and weather-related losses. The cause of loss is referred to as a peril. Even though insurance companies expect a certain number of claims, the percentage is relatively predictable as long as they insure enough geographically diverse residences.

When we purchase homeowners insurance we've transferred the risk of loss (for covered perils) to the insurance company. We intentionally retain part of the chance of loss (the deductible in the policy) to make the premium reasonable.

You can't go to your local insurance agent and expect him or her to write you a policy to cover unexpected losses on your investments. Insurance companies write policies to cover only pure risks, where there is a possibility of loss or no loss. An insurance company will not write a policy for a speculative risk, where there is the possibility of profit or loss. For example, you won't find an insurance company that offers a policy insuring against the loss of the market value on your home.

Investment risks all come down to uncertainty. If we knew with certainty whether the market was going up, down, or even staying the same, we could make truckloads of money in the market. Most investors gamble that the market will go up, and based on the past, that looks like a reasonable bet. But the market is loaded with hazards that increase uncertainty, thereby increasing our chance of loss. Compare just some of the "hazards" presented in Chapters 2, 3, and 4 to a few hazards associated with owning a home:

OWNING INVESTMENTS—HAZARDS THAT INCREASE CHANCE OF LOSS

Fraudulent accounting
Unethical management
Bad economy
Irrational behavior of investors

Owning a Home—Hazards That Increase Chance of Loss

Defective wiring
Located in flood zone
Hurricanes
Oily rags stored next to the furnace

We can reduce the chance of home loss by reducing the controllable hazards. We can correct defective wiring and dispose of those oily rags. We can buy a home that's not in a flood or hurricane zone. All of these hazards are controllable by us if we choose to avoid them. But what can we do to guard against defective accounting and sleazy management? We can lobby for reform and vote our proxies, but this does nothing to reduce the current risk of owning investments. Conflicts of interest are built into the system. How do we deal with that? As for the irrational behavior of investors, we'll never be able to figure that one out. And these are only a select few of the many hazards of investing.

Risk Management

So what do we do about market risk? Traditional risk management says there are four things we can do: avoid it, attempt to control or minimize it, retain it, or transfer it.

Avoiding Risk

If we are concerned about a plane crash, we don't fly.
If we're concerned about stock market risk, we don't invest in stock.

Controlling Risk

If we are concerned about our health, we watch our diet and exercise.

We try to minimize market risk by asset allocation and diversification.

Retaining Risk

We decide to take the risk that our $50 lawn ornament will be stolen.
We decide to invest all of our 401(K) in our employer's stock.

Transferring Risk

We buy a homeowners policy to transfer our risk of loss by fire to an insurance company.
We buy a market-linked investment to transfer the risk of loss in the market to the issuer.

Every one of us is a risk manager regardless of how little or how much we own. We don't just manage our personal tangible assets, including money and investments, but we make daily decisions that affect our health, quality of life, and our life expectancy. Some risks are impossible to transfer. We can't smoke and eat junk food every day and transfer the increased risk of heart trouble to someone else.

The majority of people with money to invest put a substantial portion into the stock market. The minority choose to deal with stock market risk by complete avoidance. Stock market risk is conventionally dealt with by retention, with an attempt to minimize and control it through diversification, asset allocation, and a long-term outlook. The problems associated with this method of risk management for stocks/mutual funds are well documented and give investors a false sense of security, especially when overall markets are unchanged or increasing as they were in the 1990s. This traditional method of managing risk is unsound. Investors are still gambling with their principal.

But there is an opportunity cost in missing out on the sometimes exceptional gains that investing in the market can provide. **The answer to this dilemma is to transfer the risk of being in the market to a third party.** When you transfer the risk of loss of your house to a third party you pay a premium, even though you hope you never have to submit a claim. When you transfer the risk of market ups and downs to a third party you continue to hope that the market goes up in the long run, even though you may not receive 100 percent of the increase. The fact that you might not get a return as high as the overall market is the "premium" you pay for the guarantee that you won't lose the principal of your investment.

If you shop for homeowners coverage with different insurance companies, you may be surprised to find a wide variation in premiums for the same coverage. Some insurance agents represent multiple companies so that they can provide their clients with more competitive rates. By the same token, protected investments are plentiful and provide a broad range of guarantees and benefits. Chapter 9 reviews some of the types of protected investments that are available today.

CHAPTER SEVEN

MAINTAINING CONTROL
OF OUR FINANCIAL FUTURE

You can never plan the future by the past.
EDMUND BURKE, POLITICAL PHILOSOPHER (1729–1797)

THE PROTECTED INVESTOR

THE ARMADILLO protects itself from its predators with armor made of small plates of bone. When attacked, it rolls itself up and becomes practically invulnerable. Since there are so many predatory risks in the investment world, like the armadillo, we need a protective shield to keep us invulnerable to them. We need to examine our goals and objectives and have reasonable expectations for returns on our investments. But before looking at possible sources for a return *on* our investment, we need to assure that there will be a return *of* our investment. We have to be constantly aware of the worst possible outcomes and of new defenses that we can use to protect ourselves while thriving in this harsh environment.

Setting Your Goals and Objectives

The first step in constructing a Protected Plan is to take a current inventory of how you shape up financially. This is basic and entails constructing a personal statement of net worth (balance sheet). List everything you own (assets) and its value in one column. List everything you owe (liabilities) in another column. The difference is your personal net worth.

When you are constructing a Protected Plan you don't need to fret over how much risk to take. Your objective is to minimize risk and achieve a reasonable return over time. If you want to take on some risk with a portion of your portfolio, I suggest that it be a relatively small amount. Stay away from individual stocks unless you want to set aside some play money for gambling. Decide in advance the maximum amount you are willing and able to lose.

Once you have listed all of your assets and liabilities, list the rate of return, if known, next to assets that generate interest, and the interest rate you are paying (Cost) next to your liabilities.

The format of your balance sheet should look something like this:

ASSETS		RETURN/COST
1ST NAT'L. BANK CHECKING	$ 5,000	0% INTEREST
1ST NAT'L. BANK SAVINGS	10,000	2.5% INTEREST
STOCK PORTFOLIO	50,000	UNCERTAIN (COMMON STOCK)
401(K)	75,000	UNCERTAIN (STOCK MUTUAL FUNDS)
CREDIT UNION IRA 3 MO. CD	20,000	3%
RESIDENCE—VALUE	200,000	UNCERTAIN
RENTAL HOUSE	70,000	UNCERTAIN
AUTO AND PERSONAL	20,000	NEGATIVE
TOTAL ASSETS	$450,000	

LIABILITIES		RETURN/COST
1ST NAT'L. BANK HOME MTG.	120,000	6.5%
2ND NAT'L. BANK RENTAL MTG.	30,000	7.5%
AUTO LOAN	7,000	1%
CREDIT CARD	5,000	14%
TOTAL LIABILITIES	$162,000	
NET WORTH	$288,000	

What you are earning on your fixed rate investments and what you are paying on your debt are vital statistics. If you have a retirement plan through your employment, know all of the investment options and be up-to-date on how you are invested. If the return is uncertain because it depends on unpredictable price movements such as the value of your real estate or your stock portfolio, note this on your statement.

■ ■ ■

Once the inventory is complete, you can think about financial goals and objectives. It's difficult to draw up a plan unless you have identified these. For many people this is the hardest part of the process and is something they have never considered. This part of the process deserves some serious introspection. Ask yourself questions like this: At what age do I want to retire? How will I fund my children's education? How much income will I need at retirement? And, what happens in the event of my death? All need to be carefully considered.

Quality of Life

Most people dream of reaching the point where they no longer have to be concerned about money issues. This means that we can meet our expenses and have arrived at the place where we can reduce or eliminate the time spent working and worrying about money.

Americans are spending more time on the job than they did twenty years ago. Our quality of life is diminishing. According to the book *The Overworked American: The Unexpected Decline of Leisure,* we are working about 170 more hours a year. We have bigger homes, more cars, and record consumption, yet our quality of life has decreased by over 50 percent since 1970, as measured by the Index of Social Health.[1] Americans use 30 percent of the earth's resources yet make up only 5 percent of the world's population. In other words, all this stuff we work so hard to acquire, much of it financed with debt, hasn't made us any happier.

Money in and of itself doesn't make us happier either. The highest income earners in the United States are doctors, yet they are among the professions that have the highest percentages of unhappy people, along with lawyers.

The average time spent shopping each week by Americans is six hours. The average time spent playing with children is forty minutes per week.[2] It has been estimated that during a person's lifetime he or she will have watched the equivalent of a year's worth of television commercials.

When we set our financial goals we need to step back and determine what we really value in life. In 1967, 83 percent of college freshmen felt that it was essential to develop a philosophy of life. In 1987 this figure dropped to 39 percent.[3] As a society we've become focused on the generation and consumption of material wealth at the cost of our own self-actualization and happiness.

And what's to keep these trends from continuing? The American people are like willing pawns in a giant economic chess game. Our children are born into a world where they are exposed to over 360,000 advertisements by the time they graduate high school.[4] Experts in marketing and psychology design ads that shape our personal needs and desires, creating the most prolific consumers in the world. We are willing to subordinate time spent with our families and our personal long-term happiness to buy whatever Madison Avenue directs.

■ ■ ■

In a Protected Plan the goal is not the attainment of a certain amount of money within a predefined time frame. This isn't a competition to see who gets there first or who can buy the most toys. Simple intermediate goals such as getting the house paid off or saving enough to help the kids with college are the primary focus.

If expenses are kept under control and we avoid the social disease of rampant consumerism, it becomes much easier to achieve the ultimate goal—financial freedom.

The Protected Plan is much more than being cheap or frugal; it's about learning to want less. It is a realization of the belief that time is much more valuable than money. More time is generated to nurture relationships, acquire insights, and experience the joy of having total freedom and control of our lives.

With the Protected Plan, our assets don't fluctuate wildly based upon a stock market that can change on a whim. Our financial well-being doesn't depend on such nonsense. We are inoculated against the emotional disease of severe depression or despair that can overtake the person who agonizes over financial issues.

Managing Expectations

At the peak of bull markets, investors believe that the gains will continue indefinitely. Surveys during the bubble of the late 1990s indicated that expectations of future annual returns soared to greater than 30 percent.

In the Protected Plan, slow and steady growth is acceptable. We avoid direct investments in the markets that put the achievement of our goals at risk. We focus on shielding our principal and finding alternatives to the traditional approach of buying individual stocks and mutual funds. We know that time-honored methods of dealing with market risk, such as diversification, asset allocation, and market timing, do not provide us with the level of protection that we need.

There is reasonable comfort in a U.S. government-backed security that pays a fixed rate of interest. But when it comes to the stock market, there is complete uncertainty. Even though we are constantly reminded to keep our long-run vision, history tells us that bear markets can wipe out years of gains in a very short time. We are not willing to shoulder this risk.

Control of Spending

The frustrating part of investment planning is that the future is unpredictable and out of our control. Choosing the appropriate way to allocate investments and selecting the particular investments to achieve our goals is more of an art than the science it sometimes appears to be. Ask 1,000 different investment plan professionals what to invest in, and you'll probably receive 1,000 different answers.

It's desirable to maintain as much control as you possibly can over the variables that affect your financial returns over time. This begins with maintaining control over spending. The amount you expend each month should on average be less than the amount of your after-tax disposable income. The difference is savings and goes right toward increasing your net worth. If you can't live beneath your means, and you depend upon credit cards and other loans to make up financial shortfalls, you will never attain financial freedom unless you receive a windfall such as a large inheritance or lottery jackpot.

Paying off Debt

One of the first things to consider in a Protected Plan is paying off personal debt. Paying off a credit card debt charging 14 percent interest gives you a guaranteed 14 percent return on your investment. Once completely paid down to zero, make sure credit cards are paid off monthly in the future, or don't use them at all. Credit card interest isn't even tax deductible and should never be used to finance spending.

Next, look at the interest rates you are paying on your mortgages and other loans. Can you earn more in a risk-free investment? If not, by paying down the mortgage or other debt, the risk-averse investor makes a guaranteed risk-free return of the percentage of interest that would have been paid on the debt.

Debt is not always a bad thing, and it doesn't always make sense to pay it down. There are times when we may end up with very low interest loans, even as low as zero percent. For example, automobile dealers frequently offer low- or no-interest loans as incentives to purchase a new car.

In order to determine whether the interest rate you are paying on your debt is too high, I suggest comparing the loan rate to the current inflation rate. If the loan rate is higher, the interest on the loan is costing you real dollars. If the loan rate is the same or lower than the inflation rate, you have a favorable debt that is actually beneficial to your financial health.

Gaining Control

Here is immediate action you can take to gain more control over your financial future:

1. Checking accounts pay very little or no interest. Keep the balance just over the amount to cover service charges. Some banks will look at a combination of checking and savings accounts for service charge calculation.
2. Use savings to pay off debt. Assure that there is a backup plan in the event emergency funds are needed. This can be in the form of an equity line of credit secured by your principal residence. Many banks offer this to their borrowers at the prime-lending rate.
3. Eliminate the stock portfolio if there are no immediate severe tax consequences.

By shifting toward paying down debt, protected investors are much more in control of their finances and are receiving a guaranteed return that is not possible to get elsewhere. Avoiding interest on the loans that have been paid off reduces expenses. The plan is simple. You pay down high-interest debt and pay the minimum toward favorable low-interest debt. Sometimes credit cards offer introductory rates with low or no interest. These can be used to pay off higher interest rate debt, but you must pay off the balances or roll the debt to another favorable card before the rate increases.

■ ■ ■

The other financial assets to consider are retirement investments. We all know the value of setting aside money today for use in the future, yet as a society, we are not doing very well at this. Chapter 10 is devoted to retirement investments.

The beauty of the Protected Plan is its inherent simplicity. Financial investments are made outside of our retirement plans only after all of our high-interest debt has been eliminated. Once this has occurred, we consider only those financial investments that are insured, guaranteed by the U.S. government or U.S. government agencies, and other alternative protected investments.

Notice I use the word "financial" investments. Other investments, such as owning a home, fit into the plan, even though it's not possible to insure that the market value will not be less when we try to sell it. Ownership of a rental home may also be a good investment, especially if you are handy and can fix up a place to increase its curb appeal and market value. Again, you don't have control over the market value, but you do have control over important factors such as determining the location of your purchase, approving qualified renters, and maintaining the property so that it continues to be attractive as both a rental and an investment.

Compare this to the amount of control you have when you buy stock in a company. Virtually none! There could be all kinds of things going on in "your" company that you are clueless about. Yet you are one of the owners. And when you buy a managed equity mutual fund you've lost what little control you do have. You've delegated your right to choose the investment to someone else.

Ongoing Plan Maintenance

Once a plan is put into action it needs to be continually updated for life-changing events that may occur. The birth of a child will probably generate a new desired goal: building a college education fund. An inheritance could create a huge windfall, or on the other hand, you might incur unexpected expenses from helping an ailing relative.

The plan can always be modified, but its basic principles remain the same. Getting out of unprotected investments should be top priority regardless of what the market is doing. This also applies to uninsured corporate bonds or corporate bond mutual funds. If you *must* hold stocks, check with your investment consultant about buying put options. These will act as insurance and protect you against massive decreases in the stock price. It does cost some money to protect yourself, but consider that we insure far less valuable items (such as automobiles) for possible unforeseen losses of value.

Review your list and ask yourself if each asset is insured against loss. The FDIC insures bank accounts up to $100,000. Government-backed securities are guaranteed by the U.S. government or agency. An insurance company guarantees insurance company annuities. Your house, rental house, and auto should be insured for loss against a number of potential hazards, including fire and theft. Every material asset you possess should be protected if at all possible. It would be a worthwhile exercise to do this not only when first implementing your Protected Plan but at least once per year.

Don't make the mistake of falling in love with your stocks or mutual funds. Remember, when the market is going down you'll be advised not to panic because "the market always goes up over the long run." This might have been true in the past, but as long as there are alternative protected investments available, why take the risk of being subject to market losses, unless your intention is to be a gambler.

The Protected Plan eliminates the problems associated with trying to time the market and all of the psychological issues relating to stocks discussed in Chapter 2. Also remember that individual investor performance is dismal relative to actual market performance, and even the professionals can't beat the market, as discussed in Chapter 1. That's why indexing has become so popular.

PART III

SMARTER AND SAFER INVESTMENTS

CHAPTER EIGHT

THE MATCHING GAME
INVESTING IN THE INDEXES

There are two kinds of investors, be they large or small:
those who don't know where the market is headed,
and those who don't know that they don't know.

WILLIAM BERNSTEIN, *THE INTELLIGENT ASSET*
ALLOCATOR (NEW YORK: MCGRAW-HILL, 2001)

BEATING THE MARKET AT ANY COST

C ONVENTIONAL investment managers have an interesting
view of risk. They are more concerned with the variation between the actual return on the money they manage
and the overall performance of the market than they are with
preserving the client's capital. Most use specific benchmarks,
such as a particular stock index, to evaluate their performance. If the benchmark stock index is up 20 percent and the
managed funds do better, the manager is deemed to have a
successful period. If the market is down 20 percent, the fund
is deemed a success if it is down anything less than 20 percent. Success is defined as beating the market, not preserving
the capital.

■ ■ ■

Endless combinations of stocks have been grouped together
to form unique indexes. An index is initially based on the total
value of a group of stocks. It provides a convenient measure for

evaluating the stock price movement of the particular group of companies.

Anyone can put together an index. Many firms construct their own distinctive indexes. You may have seen the "Dilbert" index on the Internet, which is composed of actual companies. Every working day we are continuously updated on the behavior of the most widely used indexes—the Dow, the S&P 500, and the NASDAQ.

- **Dow Jones Industrial Average (Dow)**—Dow Jones & Company has over 3,000 different indexes, but this is the most widely known. The index was put together in the late 1800s and originally consisted of twelve stocks chosen by Charles Dow. Dow invented the average as a benchmark to determine whether the overall market was going up or down. It's the oldest of the indexes. Today, the index consists of thirty "blue-chip" companies. The larger, more influential companies carry more weight when the average is calculated.
- **Standard & Poor's 500 (S&P 500)**—This is one of the most commonly used benchmarks of the overall market. It is a useful benchmark for large companies and accounts for about 70 percent of the U.S. market value. As the name implies, 500 companies make up the index. The index was invented in 1957 when technology only provided for an hourly calculation throughout the trading day. Of course today, changes in the index are calculated instantaneously. Most active mutual fund managers measure their performance against the S&P 500.
- **NASDAQ Composite**—This index includes over 5,000 companies and is one of the most widely followed and quoted indexes. Many new companies elect to have their stock traded on NASDAQ, which stands for National Association of Securities Dealers Automated Quotation

System. Many of the new high-tech and dot-com companies trade on NASDAQ, which helps to make this a volatile index. To illustrate, during the four-year period from July 30, 1998, to July 30, 2002, the index went from 1919.58 to 5046.86 and back down to 1344.19. For some investors, it was a wild ride to nowhere. Others got rich quick, and a large number who got in at the top took a hair-raising trip straight down.

BOGLEHEADS—THE ARGUMENT FOR INDEXING

John Bogle, retired chairman and founder of Vanguard Group, was instrumental in creating the first index fund to be marketed to individual investors. The Vanguard 500 Index Fund was launched two years after the birth of Vanguard in 1974. The fund, once known as "Bogle's Folly," had total assets of close to $100 billion at the end of 2000. The near-fanatical believers in index funds are proud to be called "Bogleheads" and respectfully refer to John Bogle as Saint Jack.[1]

Bogle has been a champion of low-cost investing and indexing for decades, delighting Bogleheads with his sharp criticism of stock-picking brokers and investment managers. He believes—and effectively demonstrates—that stock picking just doesn't work over the long run. Bogle says, "Beating the stock market is a zero sum game, which means it's a loser's game after costs. Indexing eliminates many of the risks associated with investing: the risks of picking individual stocks, portfolio managers and investment styles. Why not eliminate as much risk as you can?"

St. Jack realizes that there's an entertainment value in investing. He says if you have extra money, you can afford to have a funny money account. "But don't put one penny more than five percent of your assets into funny money, and track it carefully," he says.[2]

Although John Bogle retired from active management of Vanguard when he reached age 70 at the end of 1999, he has stayed busy preaching his message of fiscal responsibility and the virtues of indexing. He even wrote a book entitled *John Bogle on Investing: The First 50 Years* that was published in 2001. Excerpts from his book directly address the supposition that investment professionals can deliver superior returns:

> **Successful Fund Managers Fail**—*Fund managers, of course, are following a complex methodology. They decide on their investment strategy, evaluate individual stocks, try to determine the extent to which a company's stock price may discount its future prospects and turn their portfolios over with a passion. All of this complexity, however, has failed to produce market-beating returns. In recent years the fact has become well accepted. Not merely by academics and financial analysts who have been proving that elemental fact since time immemorial, but by the fund industry itself.*

> **All the News That's Fit to Print**—*The record hardly improves when we consider the accomplishments, published each quarter, of five investment advisers who, five and one half years ago, were asked to select and manage hypothetical portfolios for the* New York Times *based on their own complex methods of evaluation. Since then, the $50,000 that each adviser initially invested has grown, on average, to $103,500. Not bad? Not bad until you realize the measurement standard set by the* Times *grew to $156,100. Thus, the investor who chose not to use the pros gained an extra $53,000 on his initial $50,000 stake.*

> **Manager of the Year**—*I admire . . . Morningstar Mutual Funds . . . for their courage in having selected, each year since 1987, the equity fund manager of the year. The managers selected through 1997 have, after admittedly brilliant records*

prior to their selections, quickly turned nondescript. Not a single one of these managers surpassed the S&P 500 Index in the years that followed their selection.[3]

Index fund proponents claim that these funds are superior over actively managed funds for a number of reasons, including:

- The annual expenses and fees of index funds are one-tenth to one-third that of actively managed mutual funds.
- Actively managed funds, when adjusted for risk, do not outperform the appropriate index by enough to cover the cost of their higher trading costs and taxes.
- If a fund claims *higher returns* than an index, they took *more risk,* either through stock concentration or style drift (deviating from the agreed-upon parameters).
- Claims of higher returns are the result of inaccurate benchmarking (using the wrong index), which is the measurement of risk. Also, many costs of actively managed funds are overlooked, such as loads and taxes.

In Chapter 1, you saw evidence of how badly individual investors perform relative to the market. For the period 1984 to 2000, a $100,000 investment would have grown to approximately $705,000 in an index fund tied to the S&P 500 index, when adjusted for inflation. That same $100,000 would have shrunk to about $54,500 in one-year treasury bills. The average equity investor would see a value of only $42,000.[4]

When you purchase an index fund you are addressing two issues that drag down investment returns. Since most actively managed mutual funds don't do as well as the overall market, by using an index fund you know that your fund will perform in line with the overall market. Also, since index funds are not managed, the management fees and expenses for running the fund are very low. Put these two factors together, and it makes an index fund look extremely attractive compared to an actively managed fund that is attempting to beat the market.

INVESTMENT ADVISERS—THE ARGUMENT AGAINST INDEXING

"There are two kinds of investors, be they large or small: those who don't know where the market is headed, and those who don't know that they don't know. *Then again, there is a third type of investor—the investment professional, who indeed knows that he or she doesn't know, but whose livelihood depends upon appearing to know.*"

This quotation from Bernstein's book pretty much sums up why some people insist on continuing to try to beat the market. Active mutual fund managers and most financial advisers argue against indexing investment returns because their jobs are based upon giving people hope that by using a professional to manage money, superior returns will be generated with less risk.

In days gone by if you bought stock from a stockbroker, you paid a fairly hefty commission for the privilege. Today, you can buy a mutual fund directly from the fund company with no commission (no-load) and just about any number of shares of a publicly held corporation for less than ten dollars.

To survive in this environment, the investment sales and advisory business needed to convince investors that they added value to the process. They figured that investors wanted not just execution—the buying and selling of a security—but valuable advice as well. The financial services industry has reinvented itself so that investors have to pay for this advice, usually a fee of one percent to two percent of the total amount being managed. In order to justify this fee, many advisers claim to have a unique or logical system that will provide superior results.

Admitting that an index fund's performance is superior to actively managed money is analogous to saying, "Our service doesn't add any value." Most investment managers and advisers are naturally unwilling to make this admission. However, exhaustive studies on the performance of professional investors conclude that it is the investment manager's fee, not skill, that plays the biggest role in determining performance. The higher the fee, the worse the performance.

In 1992 the television show *20/20* did a news story on investment firms and their value. The story showed clips of the following three investment commercials:

- Shearson Lehman: *We're number one in investment research. Talk with us.*
- Prudential: *So for peace of mind, investment advice, and your future—Depend on the Rock.*
- Merrill Lynch: *At Merrill Lynch we know that risk can be dealt with. It can be managed.*

These commercials by the brokerage firms sound impressive, don't they? The conclusion of the *20/20* story was that despite all of the sophisticated research and the rooms filled with people in suits studying numbers, the advice that comes out of brokerage firms is so consistently mediocre that odds are you would do better picking stocks by throwing darts at the stock tables. It's hard to believe that this would be a better way to pick stocks. But the people who chart the brokerage firms' recommendations say the numbers don't lie.[6]

A college textbook, simply titled *Investments*, eloquently states this warning to students: "Not surprisingly, the efficient market hypothesis does not exactly arouse enthusiasm in the community of professional portfolio managers. It implies that a great deal of the activity of portfolio managers—the search for undervalued securities—is at best wasted effort, and quite probably harmful to clients because it costs money and leads to imperfectly diversified portfolios."[7]

SAFEGUARDING FINANCIAL ASSETS AGAINST LOSS—THE CRITICAL ISSUE

Index funds are admittedly a great tool for removing the risk of significantly underperforming the market. But this is not the goal of a risk-averse investor. The goal is to preserve capital and to protect principal from the risk of loss.

Rather than trying to beat or match the market, investors would be better served by concentrating on transferring the risk of investing to third parties. Again, attempting to control market risk by diversification and asset allocation will help to reduce market risk but won't eliminate it. Just one bear market can devastate the value of even a well-diversified portfolio.

If you held a diversified portfolio of index funds between the market high of early 2000 and July 2002, you wouldn't be very happy with your performance. Consider the performance numbers for these indexes during that period:

RUSSELL 2000	DOWN 33%
WILSHIRE 5000	DOWN 45%
S&P 500	DOWN 46%
NASDAQ COMPOSITE	DOWN 75%
AMEX INTERNET INDEX	DOWN 90%

You can see that for this period the smaller companies that compose the Russell 2000 didn't go down as much as the other indexes. Diversification certainly reduced the risk of investing in just one area, such as the technology laden NASDAQ index or the downtrodden Internet index, but if you were equally invested in each index, your portfolio would still be down by over 50 percent during this period. Each index fund has its unique characteristics with its unique risk and rate of return.

If total financial assets were allocated 60 percent stocks, 30 percent bonds, and 10 percent money market, you would have had a 30 percent decrease in financial net worth from the stock portion of your portfolio that is partially offset by the interest earned on bonds and the money market account.

You can see from this example that asset allocation and diversification reduced the amount of loss but didn't do away with it.

Risk is one of the most avoided, misunderstood, and least quantified subjects in the financial services industry. This is unfortunate, because the primary purpose of an investment professional should be the intelligent management of financial risk. Risk is always present because nobody can predict the future. Protecting financial assets against loss while achieving a reasonable rate of return should be the objective of both investor and adviser. This is the critical issue in investing, and it is being handled by many professionals with smoke and mirrors.

The index fund believers are on the right track in recognizing that it is impossible to beat the overall market except by sheer luck. Backed by volumes of financial research, index fund proponents believe they have found the Holy Grail to investment success, while professional money managers are chastised for what they are—speculators.

Here is an excerpt from "The Parable of Money Managers," an article by William Sharpe, Nobel laureate in economics:

The owner of the casino suggested a new idea. He would furnish an impressive set of rooms which would be designated the Money Managers' Club. There the members could place bets with one another about the fortunes of various corporations, industries, the level of the Gross National Product, foreign trade, etc. To make the betting more exciting, the casino owner suggested that the managers use their clients' money for this purpose.

The offer was immediately accepted, and soon the money managers were betting eagerly with one another. At the end

of each week, some found that they had won money for their
clients, while others found that they had lost. But the losses
always exceeded the gains, for a certain amount was
deducted from each bet to cover the costs of the elegant sur-
roundings in which the gambling took place.

Before long a group of professors suggested that investors were
not well served by the activities being conducted at the
Money Managers' Club. "Why pay people to gamble with
your money?"[8]

Isn't that exactly what is happening when you turn your
money over to a professional money manager? The money
manager is speculating on stocks or mutual funds without
establishing a plan for protection of the principal beyond diversification, asset allocation, and a long-term time horizon.
Sharpe's parody was about active investment managers trying
to beat the overall market. *You are actually paying someone to*
gamble with your money!

It's a pretty wacky way to accumulate wealth, yet it's still the
prevailing wisdom of our times. Index funds are designed to
closely match an underlying basket of stocks. Unfortunately,
the funds are subject to the same downward market risk that
exists with professionally managed funds. There is a better way.

CHAPTER NINE

THE PROTECTED INVESTOR
SMARTER, SAFER WAYS TO INVEST

The best way to escape from a problem is to solve it.
ALAN SAPORTA, RECORDING ARTIST
WWW.THINKEXIST.COM

TOOLS FOR TRANSFERRING RISK

I F THE TRADITIONAL methods for dealing with risk are inadequate, and the investor has placed a higher priority on preservation of capital than on trying to beat the market, what is the solution? We know there is an inherent risk when investing in the market, but what about the lost opportunity of missing out on the sometimes spectacular gains that can occur? What is a prudent, conservative investor to do?

There are money management tools that can virtually *eliminate* the risk of being in the market while still allowing for participation in any upside. Many of these tools have been significantly enhanced over the last ten years, while some have been around for hundreds of years. Some of these tools can become overly complicated for the nonmathematically inclined, but fortunately you don't have to understand all the intricacies of the ingredients to follow a recipe for dealing with risk.

HEDGING

Risk management tools are commonly referred to as *derivatives* in financial literature. They come in two flavors: *futures* (contracts for future delivery at specified prices) and *options* (contracts that give one side the opportunity to buy from or sell to the other side at a prearranged price). Futures are only used in the commodities market. Options contracts, on the other hand, are commonly used to hedge stock market-related risks.

Customized options contracts are frequently created by institutions and are traded among these large organizations. In 1973 the Chicago Board of Options Exchange (CBOE) was founded. The CBOE created standardized listed contracts that can be purchased and sold on a number of different stocks and indexes. The CBOE accounts for approximately 51 percent of all U.S. options trading and 91 percent of all index trading. The CBOE lists options on over 1,200 widely traded stocks.

An option can be fashioned on any financial instrument that fluctuates in price. In 1983 the CBOE began to trade options in the S&P 100 index. Today, options are available on just about any index, including sector indexes. Investors can effectively place insurance on their equities by using options strategies. A detailed description of how to use options as equity insurance is included in Appendix A and is highly recommended for anyone who absolutely insists on owning individual equities.

Options are an important ingredient in the development of products that allow the protected investor to participate in the market without risking principal.

MARKET-LINKED INVESTMENTS

The price of an option is based on a number of factors. The theoretical value of an option is a function of the current stock price, expected dividends, the options strike price, expected interest rates, time to expiration, and expected stock volatility. In 1973 Fischer Black, a Wall Street consultant, and Myron Scholes, assistant professor at MIT's Sloan School of Management, published their landmark article, "The Pricing of

Options and Corporate Liabilities." Today, a formula aptly called "Black-Scholes" incorporates all of these factors in the calculation. The ultimate price of an option is based on supply and demand just like a stock, but it is very likely to be close to the theoretical value.[1]

Black and Scholes came up with a way to avoid losing money in the financial markets by purchasing a mix of securities that cancel out risk. If market conditions are right, a combination of index options and bonds can be structured to give the investor the same return as the index if the market is up, but no losses if the market is down.[2]

The easiest way to illustrate how this works is with a simple example. Let's say you have $100,000 and access to a very safe investment that will generate a little over 7 percent interest. In order to assure that you have $100,000 one year from now, you would invest approximately $93,000 in the safe investment, leaving $7,000. You take the $7,000 and invest in a call option on the S&P 500 index that expires a year from now. If the market goes down by any amount, even to zero, your safe investment will still grow from $93,000 to $100,000 because of the interest. If the market increases, the option would increase in value to give you a total return in excess of $100,000. The amount in excess of $100,000 depends on the return from the option.

The higher the interest rate on the safe investment, the more money that can go into the option. The less volatile the stock market, the more option you get for the money. In a period of relatively high interest rates and stable markets, you could actually have the guarantee against loss and get over 100 percent of a positive market return. So let's say the market is up 10 percent during the period. Your return might be 12 percent, even with the guarantee against loss.

If interest rates are low, less money is allocated to the option purchase. If markets are volatile, it's a double whammy because you're getting less option for the money. Generally, higher volatility increases the cost of the option. In this case you still have the guarantee against loss, but if the market goes up, you may receive less than 100 percent of the market increase. Even though the investor may participate in only a portion of a market advance, the market-linked investment is still attractive compared to other safe alternatives.

The financial engineers who work for banks, insurance companies, and brokerage firms manufacture "market-linked" investments that provide guarantees against loss. These institutions have the ability to purchase customized options at less cost than the individual investor and therefore can provide attractive alternative investments.

As an investor, understand that when an institution offers a market-linked investment, the institution intends to be completely hedged for any market outcome. A depository bank traditionally operates by taking money in via deposits and paying a lower rate relative to the money it lends out. This difference is called a *spread*. The institution really doesn't benefit if the market heads one way or another. The institution is factoring in the spread so that it can provide stated guarantees and an attractive instrument for the investor while allowing a reasonable profit to the institution.

For risk-averse investors, market-linked investments are attractive alternatives to traditional equity and mutual fund investments. Market-linked investments that are offered by institutions fall into four main categories: certificates of deposit, corporate notes, insurance annuities, and life insurance. Even certain mutual funds now provide principal protection by building a portfolio of zero coupon bonds and individual stocks.

Market-Linked Certificates of Deposit

The market-linked certificate of deposit (MCD) is not a new invention. Big banks have offered them to large and institutional depositors for years and continue to do so. Individuals began to have access to this type of investment in 1987, although many investors still have never heard of them. The cover of a brochure for market-linked CDs has this descriptive catch phrase: "The power of money in the market. The comfort of money in the bank." This describes in a nutshell the major benefit of these investments.

The MCD is like a traditional bank CD in that it has a specific maturity date and the principal is FDIC insured. The difference is how the interest is calculated and when it is paid. Unlike traditional CDs that pay a fixed rate of interest, the MCD pays interest that is tied to the performance of a participating stock market index. If the index goes up, your investment does too. Yet, regardless of what the market does, you are still guaranteed the return of your original investment at maturity.

In the early 1990s, some MCDs were paying in excess of 100 percent of the change in the index. Due to historically low interest rates, it was common to pay a rate that was less than the change in the index during the early 2000s. When investing in an MCD, consider these factors: the index, the term, the minimum interest rate, the participation rate, averaging calculations, call provisions, existence of caps, redemption provisions, and any other special terms outlined in the MCD.

The Index

Most MCDs are tied to major indexes such as the S&P 500 and Dow Jones Industrial Average. The MCD can be tied to any index as long as the bank can purchase an option to adequately hedge the equity-linked interest payment. This includes international indexes. And as we have seen, institutions have access to custom-made options that individuals can't duplicate.

Some MCDs are based on a blend of different indexes. For example, a number of MCDs have been issued based on a composite of the Nikkei 225 (Japan), Eurostox 50 (European Union), and S&P 500.

When the MCD is issued, a date is determined for the initial index set. This is usually at the close of the offering period or the date of issue shortly thereafter. This initial index level is utilized as the base rate for determining any gain in the future. This level does not change over the life of the MCD unless the terms include a reset provision.

THE TERM
The principal and interest are paid at the maturity date. MCDs are usually issued with terms of three to ten years.

THE MINIMUM INTEREST RATE
Some MCDs guarantee a minimum interest rate at maturity regardless of how the index performs. Others have a guarantee of only the return of principal. In any event, the interest is not paid until maturity.

By including provisions that limit interest, banks can reduce the cost of their hedge and provide a product that would otherwise be impossible to issue. These provisions include the participation rate, averaging, calls, and caps.

THE PARTICIPATION RATE
This is expressed as a percentage and is multiplied by the actual percentage gain in the index to determine the percentage of gain credited to the MCD. For example, if the index is up 50 percent and the participation rate is 90 percent, a gain of 45 percent will be credited to the MCD at maturity. This rate is established when the MCD is issued and remains fixed over the life of the MCD. The rate may be higher or lower than 100 percent depending on market conditions.

AVERAGING CALCULATIONS
Sometimes the bank will average the final index over some part of the term of the MCD. The actual method of averaging varies widely between MCDs.

Some MCDs calculate the final index figure by taking an average of the index on the last day of the month three to six months prior to maturity. I have seen some MCDs calculate the final index value by taking a yearly average of the index over the life of the MCD. In periods of low interest rates, some MCDs use a quarterly average beginning right after issue.

Averaging can work to an investor's advantage or disadvantage depending on how the market behaves.

CALL PROVISIONS

A call provision in a market-linked CD gives the bank the option of cashing in your MCD before the maturity date. The bank can do this on specific dates each year at a specified rate of return known as a "call premium." For example, a five-year CD may have a yearly call provision as follows:

CALL DATE	CALL PREMIUM
ONE YEAR FROM ISSUE	20%
TWO YEARS FROM ISSUE	40%
THREE YEARS FROM ISSUE	60%
FOUR YEARS FROM ISSUE	80%

This means that the bank can return your investment at four specified dates that are outlined in the particular MCD issue along with the stated call premium. If the bank called the above MCD after two years of issue, the investor would receive $14,000 on a $10,000 initial investment. If the bank does not call the MCD in the first four years, the MCD will mature at the fifth-year anniversary. The principal will be paid in addition to any interest that may be due.

Of course, the bank will not call an MCD unless the actual index has performed better than the stated call premium. It is the bank's decision whether or not to exercise the call provision, regardless of where the index stands on the call dates.

Some MCDs issued during the Internet craze were based on an Internet-related benchmark, such as the CBOE Internet Index. The volatility of this index was so lofty that the cost of the option component of the MCD was also very high. These MCDs were typically issued with call provisions. Without a way to reduce the cost of the hedge, the MCD would have been cost prohibitive from the bank's point of view.

Call provisions are not standard. You should ask the bank representative or broker/adviser to review all the relevant terms of the MCD with you, including call features.

CAPS

A cap provides a maximum interest return to the investor. For example, a 60 percent cap means that the most a $10,000 investment will return at maturity is $16,000. Caps are another mechanism used by the bank to reduce the cost of the hedge.

Caps are not standard provisions in an MCD contract. Ask the broker or bank employee about the existence of a maximum interest return.

REDEMPTION PROVISIONS

Market-linked CDs are marketed as a "buy and hold" investment by the banks. Early redemption values differ by issuer. MCDs obtained directly from a bank may not provide for early redemptions. Many MCDs available through brokerage firms provide for early redemptions on a periodic basis (quarterly or annually) as described in the offering document. Early redemption values may be more or less than the original investment.

The actual redemption price depends on the current level of interest rates and the present value of the option that the bank has purchased. If interest rates drop, the bond component is worth more. If rates increase, this element of the MCD is worth less. The value of the option component depends on the current level and relative volatility of the index. Generally, an increasing index level and/or high volatility increases the value of the option. The option is worth less when volatility is low and/or the index is down. As the MCD approaches maturity the penalty for early redemption becomes less material. In any event, if held to maturity, investors receive at least 100 percent of their original investment.

OTHER TERMS AND PROVISIONS

There is no end to the various MCD structures that can be invented by financial engineers. Review all the terms and conditions of a market-linked CD so that you understand its benefits as well as limitations.

If an MCD has call provisions, caps, or wide averaging windows, these don't necessarily make it a poor investment. They usually come into play when interest rates are low and/or volatility is high. For example, in an up market a five-year MCD with a 50 percent cap will provide a much greater return than a traditional CD or other interest-bearing investment, along with safety of principal. The upside may not be as high as an index fund, but with the MCD you have the possibility of an above-average return without risk to your original investment.

Disadvantages and Advantages of MCDs

The market-linked CD has a few disadvantages. The gains are based upon indexes without considering any dividends. An index fund would include reinvested dividends. Dividend yields on most indexes are currently pretty low, so this isn't a big factor.

The MCD does not have the same liquidity as an index or other type of mutual fund. There is a decreasing penalty imposed by the bank for cashing out early. It should be viewed as an investment that you are willing to buy and hold until maturity.

The MCD will usually pay interest based on the increase in an index, but certain factors can reduce the rate, including a participation rate below 100 percent, averaging, caps, and call provisions. MCDs purchased outside of a retirement plan are subject to income taxes. The MCDs are taxed as if they are paying income each year, even though the earnings are not realized until maturity or redemption.

The whole tax issue can be avoided by purchasing the MCD in a retirement account such as an IRA. I've seen and heard of many imprudent investment decisions being made for the purpose of reducing or even eliminating taxes. I feel that the principal protection offered by the MCD in a down market offsets the income tax implications.

In spite of some disadvantages with these investments, the many positive features of the MCD, including the protection of principal, make it a suitable investment for part of a protected investor's portfolio. Financial professionals can guide the investor in the process of choosing specific market-linked certificates of deposit.

As an independent agency of the federal government, the Federal Deposit Insurance Corporation (FDIC) guarantees the safety of deposits, including market-linked CDs, up to $100,000 per depositor per depository institution. The FDIC insures the principal of the market-linked CD but not the "contingent" interest paid at maturity. This could be a factor if the financial integrity of the issuing bank is in question. In the late 1980s hundreds of savings and loans went out of business, costing taxpayers over $100 billion. Banks periodically get into trouble by lending too aggressively and taking unhedged bets on the direction of interest rates. It could happen again. Make sure your MCDs do not exceed $100,000 per account, and don't be afraid to cash in and lock in gains when appropriate.

The fact that the MCDs are designed to be held to maturity is a positive in that it discourages the in-and-out trading that is so easy to do with index funds. Remember that it has been proven that frequent trading actually serves to reduce returns over time.

Banks have had a challenging time training their staff to appropriately offer and explain market-linked certificates of deposit. Brokerage firms have had the most success in distributing these investments, even though the investment community hasn't fully embraced the concept. Smaller banks view MCDs as suitable for "sophisticated" investors, but few customers these days look to their bank for investment advice. In addition, it takes a long time (thirty-five to forty-five minutes) to explain all the details, according to John Soffronoff, president and CEO of the $350 million Premier Bank in Doylestown, Pennsylvania.[3]

It is likely that future distribution of these MCDs will be primarily through securities dealers. One big advantage of this is that MCDs held in a brokerage account are readily transferable and easily purchased. MCDs that are purchased directly from small to midsize banks can't be held in a brokerage account, are not transferable, and many have restrictive redemption policies prior to maturity.

Example MCD

Every MCD has its own unique terms and structures. Here is an example of an actual MCD from issue to maturity:

Prudential Savings Bank—Issuer

Five-year term
S&P 500 is underlying index
100% index participation factor
Minimum deposit—$5,000
Minimum interest—Zero
FDIC insurance—$100,000 per depositor
Issue date—June 2, 1997, S&P 500 at 846.36 on issue
Maturity date—June 3, 2002

Payment at maturity is measured by the percentage increase of the S&P 500 index from the starting index value of 846.36 at issue to the closing index value. The closing index value is the arithmetic average of the six pricing dates outlined in the CD terms. These dates are January 1, 2002, February 1, 2002, March 1, 2002, April 1, 2002, May 1, 2002, and May 29, 2002. If the calculation results in a decrease, the original investment will be returned with no interest.

The actual closing index on each pricing date was as follows:

JANUARY 1, 2002	1154.67
FEBRUARY 1, 2002	1122.20
MARCH 1, 2002	1131.78
APRIL 1, 2002	1146.54
MAY 1, 2002	1086.46
MAY 29, 2002	<u>1067.66</u>
TOTAL	6709.31

The arithmetic average of indexes on these dates is 1118.22 (6709.31 divided by 6). The interest calculation is based on the percentage increase in the S&P 500 from the initial index at issue of 846.36 compared to the closing index value of 1118.22. This equals 32.21 percent [(1118.22 – 846.36) / 846.36]. An initial investment of $10,000 generated $13,212 at maturity.

Some banks provide early redemption dates that allow the CDs to be cashed in before maturity, at a market value designated by the bank at the time of redemption. The price can be more or less than the original investment, depending upon the movement of interest rates and the index that the MCD is tied to.

My own personal strategy with market-linked CDs is to redeem when the price has gone substantially up in value over the original issue cost. The $10,000 market-linked CD principal is protected at $10,000. If the redemption value increases to $16,000, the $6,000 increase is an unrealized speculative gain and is uninsured by the FDIC. This gain could evaporate all the way back to the $10,000 base level. My strategy is to take the gain, which may be less than the appreciation of the index, and reinvest the proceeds in other secure investments where my new protected principal totals $16,000. I want my gains locked in as often as possible.

On June 1, 2000, Prudential Bank offered to redeem the CD in this example for $16,500 on an original $10,000 investment. The spot appreciation (current S&P 500 index divided by initial index set) of the index was 71.1813 percent, with the S&P 500 index at 1448.81 at that point in time. The market value of $16,500 at redemption was calculated by the bank and was based on the value of the zero coupon bond used to protect the investor's principal, plus the value of the instruments used to provide the index return. The difference between the spot appreciation of the index and the market value paid at redemption, if any, can be viewed as a penalty for early withdrawal. In retrospect, it was certainly a good time to redeem and lock in the gain.

Minimum Interest Plans

In periods when interest rates are low, you may find other curious MCD terms and structures that allow the bank to hedge its guarantee but give the investor the possibility of an above-average return. For example, on March 28, 2002, HSBC Bank issued a four-year MCD that provides a minimum guaranteed return of 11 percent (2.75% simple interest, 2.64% annualized) if held to maturity. In addition, the investor had the possibility of getting as high as 112 percent (28% simple interest, 20.67 annualized) by adding the sixteen quarterly percentage changes in the NASDAQ 100 index subject to a cap each quarter of 7 percent. In this case the minimum interest assures the investor a positive return if held to maturity but gives the possibility of an even greater return.

■ ■ ■

I believe that the MCD's primary advantage—providing market-linked returns with a guarantee against loss—more than offsets any shortcomings. For the protected investor the return *of* the investment is of primary importance. Next comes the return *on* the investment. In an up market, the investment returns on an MCD may be less than on a mutual fund or individual stocks. The protected investor accepts this as a cost of the guarantee on the principal. Also, keep in mind that most investors do significantly worse than the overall market. As a result, the return on the MCD is likely to be superior to individual stocks and mutual funds managed by the investor. Market-linked investments allow the protected investor to *comfortably* tie money to the stock market.

EQUITY-LINKED NOTES

An equity-linked note is similar in structure to a market-linked CD, but the note is guaranteed by a corporation and is not backed by the FDIC. Evaluation of a potential note investment should include enhanced due diligence on the creditworthiness of the institution that issues the note. Brokerage firms that have good credit ratings issue most of these investments. Technically, the notes are liabilities of the issuing firm, which makes the investor a general creditor of the firm.

The easiest way to evaluate the credit and default risk of investing in a market-linked note is to review the credit rating assigned to the debt securities by the two most popular bond rating companies: Standard & Poor's and Moody's. Both provide a grading system that is useful in determining whether the note is of the highest quality. It doesn't do any good to purchase a security with a guarantee against loss if the firm providing the guarantee goes out of business. More on credit ratings can be found in Appendix B. If credit risk is of great concern to the investor, it's preferable to use other market-linked investments that have a guarantee from a highly rated insurance company or FDIC-insured bank. However, notes can sometimes provide a greater selection of index choices and better opportunities for liquidity.

Equity-linked notes are referred to by many different names. They are sometimes referred to as *hybrid products* and *structured products*. In addition, the brokerage firms create their own odd-sounding acronyms like MITTS, SUNS, TARGETS, and TIERS.

In 1999 Stephen Bodurtha, vice president of customized investments with Merrill Lynch, testified before the House Budget Committee Task Force on social security. He stated, "Potential downside risk keeps many people from investing in stocks, even when long-term growth is the objective. To help with this problem, Merrill Lynch has pioneered Protected Growth investing, which combines participation in the long-term appreciation potential of growth assets, such as stocks, with protection of principal. The purpose is simple: to allow the pursuit of growth with limited risk."[4]

Merrill Lynch refers to the bulk of its equity-linked notes as MITTS. This stands for Market Index Target Term Security. Merrill typically will offer a MITTS security at $10 per unit. Once issued the securities are listed and traded on the New York Stock Exchange, the American Stock Exchange, the Chicago Board of Options Exchange (CBOE), or NASDAQ. PaineWebber and Lehman have issued notes priced and traded like bonds ($1,000 denominations). Trading is usually thin, which contributes to inefficiency and periods of overvaluation as well as undervaluation.

Salomon Smith Barney has referred to their version of equity-linked notes as "Safety First" investments. They have been issued in the form of principal-protected equity-linked certificates. The more recent versions are AAA rated by Standard & Poor's and Moody's because the principal is backed by AMBAC, the same insurance company that provides private insurance on municipal bonds.

The various index notes traded on the American Stock Exchange are listed on the web site, www.amex.com. In some cases the specifications of the notes are available, including the beginning index set. Click on the tab labeled "structured products," and then click on "index notes." Equity-linked notes that trade on the Chicago Board of Options Exchange are available at www.cboe.com. Click on the "products" tab and then click on "structured products."

Although the concept of an equity-linked note is simple, you will find that every single note has its own unique characteristics, and it is best to get some advice to determine whether any of them will help meet your own financial goals and objectives.

Equity-linked notes are not unique to the United States. They can be constructed in any country and any currency as long as the issuing company can obtain the financial instruments to adequately hedge the guarantees they are providing to the investor. In Great Britain, Merrill Lynch HSBC is offering what they call "PIP" investments, which stands for Protected Investment Product. CIBC World Markets is the dominant Canadian purveyor of equity-linked notes.[5]

According to the *ABA Banking Journal,* today's wealthy investors are more knowledgeable about investment alternatives, and financial institutions seeking to attract or retain these customers would do well to offer alternatives, including hedging strategies for individual stocks and principal-protected notes. In effect, hedging strategies mitigate risk by locking in a range of stock prices based on floor and cap levels (through exercise of put and call options). Principal-protected notes, in contrast, offer the safety of bonds. They protect the principal at maturity, while providing the upside potential of equity markets, with returns linked to the performance of equity indices.[6]

Equity-linked notes have their share of critics. Financial advisers generally have negative to neutral things to say. "They really should be pushing these in a bull market, not after a bear market," expresses Carl Carpenter, portfolio manager with Tarbox Equity. John Markese, president of the American Association of Individual Investors says, "It's hard to find ten-year time horizons where stocks have lost money. Even over seven-year stretches, the S&P has lost money only four times going back to January 1926." Even industry critic John Bogle states, "If you are skittish about the stock market, perhaps you are better off staying out of stocks altogether."[7] Market-linked CDs have been the subject of similar criticism.

It's interesting how the perspective can change as the market changes. In May 1998, in the midst of a bull market, *Money* magazine mentions the Merrill Lynch "Protected Growth" equity-linked notes in an article entitled "Is this Kind of Insurance Worth the Cost?" The "cost" referred to by the article was the fact that dividends (1.4% for the S&P 500) were not included in the calculation of index gains. In addition, there is mention that some of the notes do not offer 100 percent of the participation of the index.[8]

A little over three years later, in August 2001, *Money* did an article entitled "A Walk on the Safe Side . . . Securities with Downside Protection Are Looking Pretty Good These Days." The article mentions finance professor Zvi Bodie, a believer in equity-linked notes, who has been quoted as saying, "There is no mix of stocks and bonds and cash that will give you what you can get by investing in equity-linked notes." This positive article, by a different author than the 1998 piece about equity-linked notes, questions why we haven't heard more about them since they've been around for over six years. Quoting from the article: "Perhaps investors weren't interested in downside protection because they didn't believe the markets could go down. How times change."[9]

■ ■ ■

Equity-linked notes and market-linked certificates of deposit both offer participation in a particular market index with downside protection. Both have very similar structures and are underwritten by banks and brokerage firms.

Other institutions that offer returns tied to the market with downside protection are insurance companies. The equity-index annuity is configured differently than notes and MCDs and offers another kind of investment vehicle that works well for long-term commitments.

INSURANCE COMPANIES—EXPERTS IN EVALUATING RISK

An insurance company can cover just about any kind of risk as long as it isn't a speculative risk. Trained in the intricate nuances of statistics and probability, insurance actuaries can calculate a premium that allows the company to cover its claims and make a reasonable profit on its capital. State insurance departments closely monitor all aspects of insurance company operations, including ongoing financial health, the reasonableness of premiums, and claims processing.

Annuities

An annuity is an investment whereby you receive an income either for life or a specified number of years. There are two types of annuities: immediate and deferred. An immediate annuity is funded with a single, lump-sum payment, and the income starts soon after the investment is made, usually within twelve months after purchase. A deferred annuity is funded with a single lump-sum payment or a series of flexible payments. Distribution begins at some undetermined time in the future, typically at retirement.

Immediate annuities have very little flexibility. The investor gives up rights to the principal in return for the guaranteed payment. These are used to provide a steady fixed payment, usually for life. Deferred annuities are the more flexible and appropriate choice for most people. Many investors never actually take the guaranteed income (annuitize) their investment offers but instead take withdrawals during the distribution phase of their contract.

Annuities have favorable tax treatment when purchased outside of a qualified retirement plan. Payments into an annuity are not tax deductible, but the earnings are not subject to current taxes. Any earnings on the annuity are tax deferred until they are drawn out in the future. The IRS considers that earnings are withdrawn first and principal last for tax purposes. If a withdrawal is made before age 59-1/2, it may also be subject to a 10 percent federal tax penalty. For this reason annuities are considered as appropriate investments for retirement accumulation and as a supplementary savings mechanism for retirees.

Deferred annuities may also be subject to surrender charges by the insurance company. These charges are in addition to the 10 percent penalty that the IRS dings you for early withdrawals, which makes annuities suitable only for long-term objectives.

Annuity payments are invested in either fixed or variable accounts. Variable annuities offer a combination of mutual funds and guaranteed accounts as investment options. The insurance company does not make any warranties as to the safety of principal on the underlying investments in a variable annuity unless they are specifically identified as guaranteed investments. Because the money is placed into unprotected mutual funds, most variable annuities are not suitable for the risk-averse investor. However, if the guaranteed accounts are attractive, the protected investor can consider these options within the variable annuity.

Fixed annuities offer a solid guarantee of principal by the insurer and are appropriate for the protected investor. When you purchase a fixed annuity, the issuer guarantees you a return of principal along with a stated minimum interest rate during the accumulation phase.

Equity-Index Annuities

Another type of fixed annuity is the equity-index annuity. The returns on the equity-index annuity are tied to market indexes instead of a fixed interest rate. As a result, the equity-index annuity has greater upside potential relative to a fixed interest annuity, even though both types guarantee principal.

The financial engineers who work for insurance companies have been improving the equity-index annuity design, even as the financial markets (interest rates and volatility) have made it a more challenging environment. I expect that we will continue to see creative innovations that protect principal while providing for market-linked returns.

The more often an annuity resets and the gain is locked in, the better for the investor, especially when the market is volatile and has both up and down years. Excellent equity-linked annuities are available today that have an annual reset provision. This means that any gains are locked in yearly. With the annual reset, the worst case is that the annuity doesn't return anything for the year. This practice makes it easier to envision the protected investment process as a series of steps from year to year. Some years it's a level step where no money has been made, but no money has been lost either. Other years it's a step up as the investment grows in value. The size of this step will vary with the market. There is never a step down! The new investment base is always protected.

The modern equity-index annuity allows for the compounding of any gains on an annual basis. In addition, the annuity will offer a variety of indexes as well as a fixed interest account that returns can be linked to. For example, one of the most popular equity-index annuities allows investors to allocate funds among the S&P 500, S&P 400, Dow Jones Industrial Average, Russell 2000, and a fixed account with competitive interest. Within thirty days after each anniversary date the investor can reallocate funds among these five choices. Since the funds are in an annuity this is a tax-free transaction.

Equity-index annuities do not currently give 100 percent of the increase in a particular index without some sort of modification or cap. Modifications may include calculating the gain based on an average rather than on the point-to-point method. Under the *point-to-point method* a "margin" may be deducted from the calculated gain or any gain may be reduced by a participation rate of less than 100 percent. The cap would put a maximum on the amount of the gain in a particular period. These factors change as the financial markets change.

Approximately one half of all annuity assets are in qualified plans.[10] If you place an annuity in a qualified plan such as an IRA, you are taking advantage of unique investment guarantees that the annuity can provide, which are not available with other investments. Even market-linked CDs and equity-linked notes don't have features like an annual reset provision and automatic compounding. By their very nature, equity-index annuities are long-term investments that are very suitable for retirement plans such as IRAs, SEPs, Keoghs, and 401(K)s.

The modern equity-index annuity does not have an up-front sales charge, so 100 percent of the money that is placed in the annuity goes to work for the investor. The insurance companies usually have a decreasing surrender charge or penalty for early withdrawals. The surrender charge period generally varies from five to fifteen years. The policies with the longer surrender periods should provide relatively better benefits. Be sure to compare policy terms and stated benefits to determine who is offering the best plan. A professional who specializes in protected investments should be able to do this for you. Most policies allow the owner to draw out up to 10 percent each year without a company-imposed penalty. If you are under 59-1/2, there will be the 10 percent IRS penalty to contend with.

Before investing in any insurance company product, make sure the company is financially strong. A. M. Best and Weiss Ratings assign grades to insurance companies based on financial strength and ability to meet obligations to policyholders. In addition, Standard & Poor's and Moody's assign ratings on insurance company debt. See Appendix B for rating information.

I read an article on equity-index annuities that made an interesting analogy. Here is an excerpt:

> *Another way to look at equity index annuities would be to walk into a Las Vegas casino and see two blackjack tables. Table one is your usual blackjack game where you place your bet and, if you win, you get 100 percent of your bet from the casino. But if you lose, they take 100 percent of your money. Table two is called equity index blackjack. The only difference is that when you win, you get 60 to 70 percent of the bet. But when you lose, the casino does not take your money. Which would you rather play?*[11]

I'd like to add that when you win on the equity-index table, your winnings could be compounded without any risk of losing what you have already made.

Upside without the Downside

In the early 1990s National Home Life (now called Peoples Benefit Life) issued an equity-index annuity with the return based on the five-year performance of the S&P 500 index. The policy provided for the higher of 100 percent of the increase in the index or a minimum return of 3 percent per year over five years. There was a cost of 5.75 percent to buy the policy and a five-year minimum commitment.

A $10,000 investment in the policy on the first of April 1994 resulted in a net investment of $9,425 after the sales charge. Therefore, the minimum value of the contract five years later was $10,926 ($9,425 compounded at 3% per year). The S&P 500 index on the first business day in April 1994 was 438.92. Five years later on April 1, 1999, the index was at 1335.18. The index more than tripled over the five-year period. As a result, on April 1, 1999, the value of the account grew to $28,652 using this point-to-point methodology.

At this stage the investor could cash out, transfer to another account, or commit to another five years under the same terms without paying a sales charge. This value was now locked in and couldn't decrease regardless of what happened to the market subsequent to this reset date. Therefore the minimum guaranteed value in April 2004 is $33,215 regardless of where the index closes at that time.

I gave a talk in front of a group of investment brokers in late 1993 that was suitably entitled "Stocks Suck." I reasoned that it made no sense to be in stocks or mutual funds when there were alternative investments available that provided the possibility of the upside of the market, a guarantee against loss, and even a small minimum guaranteed return. Why mess with the stock market when this is available?

The feedback was less than enthusiastic. Here are sample comments: What about the dividends on the index? Isn't 5.75 percent too high a cost to get in? When has there been a five-year period when the market wasn't up? Wouldn't a mutual fund give a higher return? There was very little worry about the possible downside of the market but lots of concern about not doing as well as the market. I argued that these kinds of investments remove the gambling aspect of stock market investing for very little cost. Most felt that this wasn't a troubling factor because historically the market has always increased if given enough time.

Unfortunately, this particular annuity is no longer offered. Of course, whenever a return is tied to the market, remember that past performance is not necessarily indicative of future results.

Averaging Is Not Always a Bad Thing

Using a daily average to calculate an investor's possible gain does not always reduce the return. It depends on how the market behaves in the period of averaging.

Unforeseen events such as the tragic day of September 11, 2001, when terrorists struck America can have a dramatic affect on the market. The stock markets closed and then reopened on September 17. The market dropped sharply in this first week following the attack. After this week of big losses the market began to rebound sharply, but by September 2002, the market was lower than the lows of a year earlier.

A contrast between some of the major indexes on September 25 of these two years is as follows:

	SEPT. 25, 2001	SEPT. 25, 2002	PERCENT CHANGE
S&P 500	1003.45	819.29	−18.3%
DOW JONES	8603.86	7683.13	−10.7%
S&P 400	417.66	402.66	− 3.6%
RUSSELL 2000	393.79	356.58	− 9.4%

An annuity with a point-to-point method of calculating the gain with an annual reset would provide no return to the investor during this period because there was no gain to share in. That's the bad news. But the good news is that the investor wouldn't have to share in any of the losses either. So for this one-year period the point-to-point annuity investor had a return of zero.

For annuities using daily averaging a dramatically different picture results. The beginning index set is the same, but the daily averaging actually served to benefit the investor in this case. Take a look at these figures:

	SEPT. 25, 2001 (INDEX SET)	ONE YEAR DAILY AVERAGE	PERCENT CHANGE
S&P 500	1003.45	1055.00	+ 5.1%
DOW JONES	8603.86	9543.82	+10.9%
S&P 400	417.66	486.86	+16.6%
RUSSELL 2000	393.79	454.31	+15.4%

An annuity with a daily averaging methodology of calculating the gain actually generated a gain to the investor during this period when the market was down significantly on a point-to-point basis. Depending on the insurance company and the original issue date of the policy, this gain was reduced slightly by a participation rate or index margin. For example, Midland National Life policies issued on September 25, 2000, indicated a 100 percent participation rate and a 1 percent index margin on the Russell 2000 index for daily averaging policies for the one-year period ending September 25, 2002. As a result, the investor in the Russell 2000 index received a 14.4 percent (15.4% – 1%) return for this year. This gain was locked in regardless of future index performance. The investor actually had a nice positive return in a year that the Russell 2000 index was down 9.4 percent!

Most policies allow the investor to change the allocation of money between indexes if so desired for the next yearly period, including a fixed interest option that is not tied to the market. I always like to have a small portion in the fixed account so that there is at least some increase from the previous year.

■ ■ ■

Depending on how the numbers fall, one calculation method may provide far superior results to another. Averaging would have reduced the return significantly in the point-to-point example for the five years ending in 1999 because the market pretty consistently increased during this period. But the point-to-point method contains the risk of giving up prior gains during the calculation period.

Another popular interest crediting method is called the *high-water mark look-back.* Account values are locked at their highest level as determined by a policy anniversary measurement. However, before future earnings may be added, the market must totally recover from any downturn. Therefore, if the index immediately drops, it must fully recover from the loss during the calculation period before getting into positive territory.

In times of tremendous volatility averaging may be the better way to go. In any event, the more often the gain gets "locked in" and the index reset, the better in a volatile market. We want to participate in the gain in the up periods and avoid the pain in the down periods. The equity-index annuity allows us to do this.

If there is enough money involved, multiple equity-index annuities with diversified issue dates may make sense. Gains are usually calculated on a policy year basis. So the issue date determines the annual reset date and the beginning index for determining the following year's performance. September and October are historically considered the "danger" months for being in the market. If this trend continues, these are good months to include in your time frame for purchasing an equity-index annuity that uses averaging.

It also makes sense to consider annuity policies with different methods of calculating the gain (point-to-point versus averaging) for diversification. One may provide far better results compared to the other in different market environments.

Equity-Index Life Insurance

If you own any life insurance that has a cash value, you may want to consider converting the policy to equity-index life insurance instead. I believe that, strictly speaking, life insurance should be purchased primarily for death protection. Term insurance, which generates no cash value, provides a death benefit at the lowest possible cost. Policies with cash values include whole life, universal life, variable life, and equity-index life insurance. If a policy that has a cash value is purchased, it is an investment in addition to providing the death benefit.

For short-term needs, cash value life insurance is a terrible investment. Returns can actually be negative if the policy isn't held for a certain period of time. However, if life insurance is needed to meet long-term objectives and you are saving for distant needs such as retirement, guaranteed cash value life insurance can be viewed as a reasonable low-risk investment. This applies especially to individuals with high tax rates who have a need for the insurance. Current tax laws permit tax-free accumulation of earnings inside a life insurance policy.

Cash value life insurance has been a popular investment mechanism with many people over the years. But in 1979 the Federal Trade Commission announced results of a multiyear study that showed returns on whole life policies held for twenty years or more were averaging only 2 percent to 4.5 percent per year. This came out when interest rates had soared as inflation skyrocketed.

Around 1980, the concept of comprehensive financial planning and having a trained financial planner recommend a course of action in line with an individual's goals and objectives was becoming popular. Planners were recommending that people borrow large amounts from their policies or even cancel their policies to invest in other areas, including money markets that were paying over 10 percent at that time. Insurance companies have been scrambling ever since to offer more competitive policies in an attempt to regain the confidence of the consumer.

In 1967, according to the Bureau of Labor Statistics, about 44 percent of households used a personal life insurance agent. In 1988 this figure had dropped to 32 percent. The United States had 252,000 agents in 1973 and only 190,000 in 1998. Aside from a brief surge in the 1980s caused by the introduction of universal life policies, the number of insurance policies sold has fallen annually over the past twenty years. Obviously the industry and its agents have yet to regain the full trust and confidence of the consumer, even though the products now offered by the industry are superior to those issued in the past.

The universal life policy offers tremendous flexibility as compared to the old whole life policies. The policy owner, within certain guidelines, can alter the premium payment and the death benefit in response to changing needs and circumstances. The insurance company can change the mortality (probability of death) charge as trends change. This is good for the consumer if people are living longer because this cost would decrease. The company can also change the interest that is credited based on changes in interest rates, usually with a guaranteed minimum.

Variable universal life allows the policy owner to invest the cash value in separate subaccounts that are not guaranteed by the insurance company. These separate accounts include mutual funds, and there is no guaranteed minimum return. The investment risk falls on the shoulders of the policy owner.

Equity-index life is actually a form of universal life. Policies provide for a guaranteed minimum interest rate, a current interest rate, and a bonus rate linked to the performance of the S&P 500 index. The guaranteed minimum rate is usually in the 2 percent to 3 percent area. The current interest rate is either the same as the minimum or a higher rate declared by the company. The bonus rate is calculated by a formula based on the one-year performance of the S&P 500. This number is multiplied by an index factor, which can change yearly.

If there is no bonus interest, the policyholder is still getting a return that is only slightly less than would be received in a traditional universal life policy. Over the long run the equity-index policy is likely to provide above-average returns in some periods and credit only the guaranteed minimum return in others. The concept appeals to me. Each year the value is increasing regardless of how the market performs.

The notion of partially participating in an up market and locking in the gain while having a guaranteed minimum rate of return is appealing to risk-averse investors. They are happy to participate partially in the up side as long as there is absolutely no participation in down markets. In periods of extreme volatility the market may drop dramatically in one period and increase impressively in another. It's nice to completely avoid the free falls but benefit when times are good.

I want to emphasize that equity-index insurance works best when there is a need for the death benefit and the owner is in a high tax bracket. Some people buy cash value life insurance as a means of forced savings. Life insurance cash values should be viewed only as a supplement to an investment plan. I've seen situations where a person is overinsured because of placing too much trust in the advice of an aggressive insurance agent.

BE WARY OF SOME PRINCIPAL-PROTECTED INVESTMENTS

The horrendous losses suffered by investors in the early 2000s have created opportunities for financial marketers to create many products that protect principal and come in all shapes and sizes. Beware of products that advertise principal protection but include contingencies on receiving the protection. I've seen products that advertise protection, but only in the event of your death or disability. Other products will have an attractive minimum guaranteed rate, but require that you take out a limited amount of principal over time at a very low rate in order to receive the protection.

Variable annuities with a guaranteed income rider are often misunderstood or misrepresented. They will guarantee a high rate such as 6 percent. You pay an extra fee for this rider each year. The problem is that in order to cash in on the guarantee you have to annuitize the contract over many years at a very low interest rate. The risk-averse investor should avoid variable annuities. They have relatively high fees and are most suitable for risk-tolerant mutual fund investors seeking tax deferral. The rider gives the purchaser of the annuity a false sense of security.

There are also principal-protected mutual funds that offer a period of time in which the principal is protected. These funds generally invest in a combination of zero coupon bonds and a managed portfolio of equities. Be wary of possible high annual expenses (over 2 percent) and sales charges. Relative to market-linked CDs and notes, as well as equity-linked annuities, the principal-protected mutual funds are a poor choice.

You may also run across other investments that sound like they are principal protected but have downside risk. An equity-linked product called a *reverse-convertible* is marketable to investors in periods of low interest rates. These securities provide double-digit interest returns, but the investor takes on the risk of being delivered the underlying equity or index. This means if the index or security is down significantly, the investor will lose money. Be sure that your investments are principal protected even if the underlying index or equity drops to zero.

WHY HAVEN'T I HEARD OF THESE BEFORE?

In the European Union and Japan individual investor demand for equity-linked investments has soared. If you venture into any of Banque Generale du Luxembourg's forty branches across the Grand Duchy, you will find posters promoting Protected Sector Notes. "Energize your portfolio!" they urge, with the participation in the gains of an international basket of leading equities while providing the investor with principal protection.

At the counter, leaflets promoting Banque Generale du Luxembourg's array of protected products are available. Open a copy of the local newspaper, *Luxembourg Wort,* and you will find advertisements for equity-linked debt products being promoted by most European banks. It's a pattern being repeated across Europe and Japan.[12]

Interestingly, the first publicly traded index-linked note, issued in 1991, wasn't offered by a bank or brokerage firm, but through the government of Austria as a five-year bond linked to the S&P 500 index.

Market-linked investments have been available in the United States since the early 1990s but relative to the overall investment universe have been nothing more than a niche product. One reason for this is that investors and their advisers did not see the need for a product that provided protection against loss. The average investor underestimated the risk of investing in the stock market until the bear market of the early 2000s shocked everyone into reality.

Another factor inhibiting the growth of market-protected products in the United States has been distribution. Equity-index annuities and insurance are purchased through insurance agents. These are not securities but are considered fixed products. Only licensed insurance agents may sell them. Only one in twenty insurance agents has ever sold an equity-indexed product. There are many variations and features of indexed insurance products, and many agents don't understand them.

Registered representatives of brokerage firms sell market-linked notes and CDs. These are considered securities. The very premise of guaranteed principal protection is at odds with the traditional teachings of risk management, so many brokers and advisers discredit them as illegitimate investment candidates. In addition, the trend with investment advisers is toward charging fees for advice in lieu of commissions. A fee of 1 percent per year for five years in a managed portfolio is much greater than a one-time commission of 1 percent or 2 percent that a broker makes from the sale of a five-year note or MCD.

You are sure to hear more about protected products as time goes on and investors demand better protection of their hard-earned savings. Insurance agents and registered representatives who want to be of service to the risk-averse investor will have to invest the time to become adequately trained in the nuances of protected investments.

GETTING THE HELP YOU NEED

Depending upon your situation, you may need the expertise and guidance of others when you are implementing a plan to protect your assets. If you are just starting out and saving for your first house, the simple plan of keeping expenses under control relative to your income is your first priority. Stay away from credit card debt, and get the highest interest rate you can with your cash savings. There are thousands of banks and credit unions in the country. You may be able to double or triple your interest by doing a little comparative shopping.

Financial Professionals

Financial professionals who can help you with the planning and implementation of your protected strategy include the following:

- **Certified Public Accountants**—Experienced CPAs have a natural tendency to be conservative and are ideally suited to help you construct a plan of protection as well as help you with tax planning issues. Some CPAs are also trained as Personal Financial Specialists. It takes a lot of training and study to become a CPA, indicating a dedication to the profession.
- **Financial planners**—Anyone can call himself or herself a financial planner. No license is needed. A Certified Financial Planner (CFP) or Chartered Financial Consultant (ChFC) has been trained in all aspects of financial planning and passed a regimen of nationally administered examinations on investments, taxation, estate planning, and risk management.
- **Insurance agents and stockbrokers**—Many financial planners also have an insurance license and a brokerage license. The examination process is less intensive than the professional designation programs.

- **Investment advisers**—Investment advisers charge a management fee based on the amount in an account, or an hourly fee for giving advice. There is no exam or special training required at the federal level to become a registered investment adviser.

It's a challenge to find one professional who can assist you with all aspects of a Protected Plan. For example, a CPA may be able to help construct a plan, but generally you'll need an insurance agent or broker to show you the various protected investments that are available. In this case the CPA can help with the comparison and help analyze and select the best-protected investments for your situation.

If you can find a professional who agrees to help you implement your strategy without trying to sell you on their "unique" mutual funds, stock management program, or other unprotected investments, you may have found a valuable resource. Shop around. Check out their experience, education, and professional background. The adviser should have experience and earned at least one professional designation such as CPA, CFP, or ChFC. Try to avoid the slick sales types and find someone you can freely communicate with who is patient enough to explain how things work.

I would be sure to work these two questions into the discussion with a financial professional:

1. How often do you utilize market-linked certificates of deposit, equity-linked notes and annuities, as well as equity-index life insurance?
2. What kind of planning strategies and investments would you use for a conservative investor concerned about risk of loss, but also concerned about missing out on possible stock market gains?

The answers to these questions should tell you whether you are going to receive real help with your investment plan that effectively manages risk, or the same old stale advice. You can get the insurance agents and brokers to research the protected investments their firms offer and put together a plan yourself. They will receive some sort of compensation if you purchase the investment through them, so you shouldn't have to be concerned about paying an additional fee for the information. In any event the first priority for the risk-averse investor is to make certain that the portfolio is fully safeguarded against loss.

CHAPTER TEN

INVESTING FOR RETIREMENT

Go confidently in the direction of your dreams.
Live the life you have imagined.

HENRY DAVID THOREAU, *WALDEN, 1854*

WE'RE GETTING OLDER, BUT ARE WE GETTING WISER?

IN 1900, 4 percent of Americans were age 65 or older. In 2000, 13 percent were 65 or above. By 2030 the Census Bureau projects that the figure will increase to 20 percent. This demographic trend will have well-documented negative effects on our social security system as the baby boomers begin to reach retirement age in 2010. Many argue that this trend will also create a volatile environment for the stock market as funds are spent or shifted to safer investments as people get older.[1]

Corporate stocks are the investment of choice for retirement plans. As a matter of fact, over 50 percent of the value of traded U.S. equities is now held in retirement accounts, and this number is growing. We trust and count on the market to help us accumulate a sufficient sum to allow us to retire comfortably.

We used to depend heavily on traditional pensions for our retirement income. The employer would provide a guaranteed retirement benefit based on a formula that factored in the number of years of service and salary. After twenty-five or thirty years of service, the employee would receive a reasonable retirement income to help supplement social security.

Most employers set aside money for this liability and took on all of the investment risk. However, there were a few bad apples.

After seven years of congressional debate, President Ford signed the Employee Retirement Income Security Act (ERISA) in 1974. Tragic tales of pension benefits wiped out by bankruptcies, mergers, and unsavory business practices prompted the laws, which stipulated that companies with pension plans had to follow certain basic rules, including actually setting money aside for pensions. Corporations have lots of flexibility in interpreting the rules, as described in chapter 3. The law also allowed individuals who were not in a traditional pension plan to set up their own retirement savings account with special tax benefits. This marked the beginning of the Individual Retirement Account (IRA).

In 1982 the Internal Revenue Service launched a public policy campaign to encourage people to save for their own retirement through before-tax payroll deductions called 401(K) plans. In a separate ruling the IRS liberalized the IRA rules to allow individuals to contribute up to $2,000 per year, including employees already in corporate pension plans. These initiatives were the main triggers to the explosive growth of the mutual fund industry. At the market peak in 1999, upwards of 75 percent of the $1.8 trillion that workers held in 401(K) accounts was invested in equities.

Today, the statistics and trends are sobering: more than 50 million workers—about half the workforce—have no pension coverage whatsoever. They have neither a traditional, employer-run pension plan to provide checks after retirement, nor a personal tax-deferred savings account such as an IRA or 401(K) plan. For small businesses, where only 25 percent of workers are covered by some sort of retirement plan, the problem is particularly acute.[2]

To make matters worse, over 50 percent of America's workers that have a 401(K) cash out when they change jobs—rather than rolling those savings over to an IRA or another 401(K)—and therefore pay taxes on the proceeds as well as a 10 percent tax penalty for withdrawing the money before age 59-1/2.

Even those who are setting aside money for retirement are doing a poor job of it. From 1983 to 1998, when the S&P index rose an astounding 774 percent, the most fortunate retirement savers—those ages 47 and over with $1 million or more in net worth—saw their retirement wealth grow by only 44 percent.[3]

Sources of Retirement Income

The main sources of retirement income are social security, benefits from pensions, retirement savings, and other investments.

- **Social security**—As many a retiree will desolately attest, it is almost impossible to make ends meet on a social security check alone. It should be viewed only as a supplement to retirement income. If you were born after 1937 and plan to retire with full social security benefits at age 65, you'll find that you may have to wait as long as age 67 to receive full benefits. This change was put into place to help strengthen the system.

- **Pensions**—This is a benefit provided by certain businesses where the employer, not the employee, makes the contributions. This type of plan is being used less and less as employees are encouraged to save and provide for their own retirement. Only 22.3 percent of the workforce is covered by a traditional pension plan, about half the percentage covered in 1975.[4]

- **Retirement savings**—This area includes accumulated savings from payroll deduction plans such as 401(K)s (for profit entities), 403(B)s (educational and certain nonprofits), and 457s (government). Profit-sharing plans, money purchase plans, IRAs, and Roth IRAs fall in this category along with many other lesser-known salary deferral plans. Nonqualified deferred annuities also fall into this category.

- **Other investments**—These include securities and assets not specifically allocated toward retirement. Personal assets would fall under this category along with the value of the personal residence. Your home can be a source of retirement income, usually as a last resort, through such things as creative sale and leaseback transactions, and reverse mortgages.

You are fortunate if you are in a position to receive both social security and a noncontributory pension because the old-style pensions are becoming rare. For investment retirement planning, we will concentrate here on retirement savings—money specifically allocated for retirement—which usually receives favorable tax treatment. We've already seen that 50 percent of active workers have no retirement plan. Those who do usually have a 401(K) or 403(B) plan.

The Protected Investor and the 401(K)

Most people who have made provisions for retirement own two major investments: their house and a 401(K) or other retirement savings account. A house can stabilize living costs and give inflation protection. The 401(K) and other salary deferral plans are great ways to save for retirement, and investors should take advantage of them to the maximum extent possible. Money set aside for retirement via payroll deduction is exempt from federal and sometimes state income taxes. Some employers match contributions up to a certain percentage. This is a valuable employee benefit that should be taken advantage of, even if the match is with company stock. Take the security if it's free, but as a risk-averse investor never direct 401(K) contributions into company stock unless you plan to sell the stock as soon as the company allows.

About 2,000 U.S. companies offer their own stock as an investment option in these plans in addition to mutual funds. Some of these corporations—including many large employers such as Coca-Cola, Proctor and Gamble, and (formerly) Enron —have essentially forced 401(K) participants to invest in company shares by issuing them as the employer's matching contribution. A survey by the Employee Benefits Research Institute showed that 18.6 percent of the average 401(K) plan balance was held in the employer's stock in 2001. For companies with more than 5,000 employees, the figure was a whopping 25 percent.[1] That even defies traditional diversification strategies of not putting more than 5 percent of investments in one company's stock.

Even without a matching contribution, the 401(K) is an excellent retirement savings tool if used properly. The earnings on the investments accumulate tax deferred. Taxes are paid when you draw funds out at retirement.

The big challenge for a protected 401(K) investor is selecting investment options that provide a reasonable opportunity for growth without risking principal. The employee cannot select investments outside of those provided in the plan by the employer. The employee may have many investments to select from, but they usually consist of variations of stock funds, bond funds, and money market funds. Money market funds are low yielding but usually safe. Bond funds can perform well at times but can actually lose money during periods of rising interest rates, when the value of bonds decreases. The risk with stock funds is certainly self-evident.

The risk-averse investor is left with very few attractive choices. A money market or ultra-short bond fund may be the best available option. Some employers offer a guaranteed interest option through an insurance company that pays an attractive rate compared to the money fund. Very few offer protected market-linked alternatives.

According to the Bureau of Labor Statistics, the average

employee stays with his or her employer for a little under three years. One strategy for the risk-averse investor is to roll over the accumulated value of the 401(K) to a self-directed IRA upon termination from the current employer. Be sure to establish the IRA before the money is requested so that the funds can be directed to the new trustee. The self-directed IRA can provide a whole array of protected products, including market-linked CDs, notes, and equity-index annuities.

Approximately 95 percent of 401(K)s offer loans to participants. Research indicates that about 18 percent of 401(K) holders borrow money from their 401(K).[5] It's generally not a good idea to borrow money designated for retirement, but some people seem unable to invest for a long period of time. If the loan provision in a 401(K) is used, then upon termination of employment, the money should be transferred to the new employer's 401(K). Loans are not available on IRAs.

There is an advantage to borrowing money from the 401(K) for a down payment on a first house, but cashing in or borrowing money from retirement funds for a big-screen TV is another story. You should be aiming to accumulate a *minimum* of ten times your last annual working salary in retirement funds by age 65 in order to generate a target of 75 percent of your accustomed income over the last twenty years of life expectancy. For example, someone accustomed to making $50,000 a year should have at least $500,000 accumulated at retirement. The average retiree in 2002 left the employer with approximately $115,000 in his or her 401(K).

It's critical to start saving as early as possible for retirement. Even if you can only save a small percentage of your income, it will grow tax deferred and be compounded over time. A solid foundation will be developed that you can add to in increasing amounts over the years.

Two important factors that we can control in saving for retirement are both the amount of money we sock away and the amount of time the money is invested. Another factor in determining how much we'll have at retirement is the rate earned on the investments. Most of us give up control of this factor by investing in unprotected equity mutual funds in a 401(K). All it takes is one bad year to wipe out years of accumulation. For example, let's say you achieve a 10 percent return over ten years on a $10,000 yearly retirement investment. If in year eleven the market drops by 40 percent, all of your gains of the previous ten years are lost. You end up with less money than if you had put it under the mattress.

Market- or Equity-Linked Investments in the 401(K)

Market-linked certificates of deposit as well as equity-linked notes are usually purchased in a brokerage account. Each has a minimum investment of $2,000 to $5,000. This makes it difficult if not impossible to purchase these kinds of securities in your typical salary deduction 401(K) plan. However, there is a way to overcome this obstacle if the employer offers a self-directed 401(K).

As mentioned earlier, the self-directed 401(K) can allow employees to purchase any security, including individual stocks, bonds, mutual funds, CDs, and so on. Only about 10 percent of employers currently offer this option to their employees. On the one hand, the plan sponsors have a fiduciary responsibility to provide diversified investment alternatives in their employees' 401(K) plans. On the other hand, the employer has the fiduciary duty of prudence in the selection and retention of investment choices.[6] Many smaller professional firms in which most workers are fairly high net worth investors use self-directional 401(K)s. A lot of these employees are interested in riskier strategies such as trading stocks. However, these plans can be used for protected, conservative strategies too.

Plan sponsors can and should limit the range of investments available in self-directed accounts. If investments are limited to

FDIC-insured CDs and other insured or very safe alternatives such as AAA rated government-backed securities and insured equity-linked notes, then the employer is properly handling their fiduciary responsibility. This gives their risk-averse employees some viable options to choose from, while not allowing unlimited investment options—including the purchase of high-risk stocks, which may not be suitable for accumulating money for retirement.

A self-directed 401(K) will cost each participant between $25 and $100 in additional administrative fees. It really isn't cost effective for the employee until this charge becomes a reasonable percentage (less than 1%) of total investments placed in this option. Because of this additional cost and the fact that CDs, notes, and government-backed securities are not suited for payroll deduction due to minimum investment requirements, the employee should only participate in the self-directed 401(K) option with $10,000 or more.

When offered in a 401(K), equity-index annuities can be purchased in increments as low as $100 per month. Unique guarantees and provisions, such as the annual reset, make equity index annuities attractive retirement investments.

In order to offer employees the additional choices of a self-directed account and equity-index annuity along with the standard fare of mutual fund options, the employer may need the services of a third-party administrator to allow more flexible investment choices. The additional fees for a custom plan are reasonable given the level of service provided. Employees are happier with the greater quality of investment options, and employers gain from providing a better benefit to employees. In addition, the employer as a fiduciary is prudently carrying out their responsibilities by providing protected investment options for risk-averse employees.

Employers may have other programs besides the 401(K) that are attractive to the risk-averse investor. This includes certain types of employee stock purchase plans.

Employee Discount Stock Purchase Plans

Most publicly held corporations offer a package of benefits, including health, retirement, 401(K), and employee stock purchase plans. Some of the stock purchase plans are well suited for the risk-averse investor, and the employee should participate to the maximum extent allowed by the employer. However, the protected investor should completely avoid *holding* employer stock and dispose of it immediately after purchase.

The employee stock purchase plan allows employees to purchase company stock at a discount. A typical plan allows employees to apply up to 10 percent of their gross salary toward the purchase of employer stock. At the end of a designated period, the money is used to purchase stock at a discount based on the lower of either the beginning or ending price (usually three or six months).

What makes this attractive to protected investors is that once the purchase is made they may sell the stock if they so desire. And that's exactly what the employee should do—sell immediately. Once the stock is in the name of the employee it becomes an unprotected investment and is subject to the usual risks associated with all other stocks.

The percentage return on this employee benefit can be substantial. For example, if the stock went from $50 at the beginning of the period to $40 at the end of the period, employees would pay $34 a share for the stock (85% of $40) assuming a 15 percent discount. If employees sold the stock immediately, they would have made $6 per share, or 17.6 percent. Assuming that this was for a six-month period and the money was put in the plan equally over six months, the annual rate of return works out to over 70 percent!

It could even get better. If the stock price went from $40 to $50, employees would pay $34 per share but immediately sell at $50 for a $16 profit per share, or 47 percent gain. On an annual basis the actual return in this example is over 180 percent. And this is without gambling.

I have to reiterate that the stock must be sold immediately after purchase to realize these gains without any exposure to market risk. The only way employees would be at risk is if the employer went bankrupt during the accumulation period. If this is even a remote possibility, don't participate in the plan.

I've met with hundreds of people over the years who had this kind of plan as an employee benefit and didn't participate. Most of those who did usually didn't put in the full amount possible and ended up holding the stock as a long-term investment. Participation in these plans is something you have to find a way to do, even if it means delaying the payment of higher-interest debt. You can use the proceeds from the stock sale as a lump-sum payment toward the debt later.

Government-Backed and Private Mortgages

Mortgages are frequently used as part of the fixed income component of a retirement plan. U.S. government-backed mortgage securities usually pay attractive interest compared to other safe income-oriented investments. A government agency guarantees interest and principal, which gives these investments the highest possible credit rating.

An investor in this type of security doesn't have to worry about whether the interest and principal will be paid, but there is a concern about the timing of the principal payments. When interest rates go down, people refinance their mortgages, and you may get the principal of your investment back sooner than you would like. The money comes back, and you then have to reinvest in a lower interest rate environment. The opposite is also true. When rates go up it may take longer than you would like to get your principal back, so you may miss opportunities to reinvest at higher rates. A good financial adviser can purchase mortgage-backed securities that minimize these risks, which the financial industry calls *prepayment* and *extension* risk. These investments go by names such as Ginnie Mae (Government National Mortgage Association), Fannie Mae (Federal National Mortgage Association), and Freddie Mac (Federal Home Loan Mortgage Corporation).

One way to minimize these risks is to control the mortgage process yourself. You can write in prepayment penalties that will help offset the annoyance of getting the principal back faster than expected. In addition, you could put in a "balloon" provision, which makes the whole mortgage come due in a certain period of time, to control extension risk.

With a private mortgage you are depending on the value of the real estate to back the mortgage for security against credit risk, instead of a government-backed guarantee. The protected investor will want the owner to have significant equity in the property before making a loan. There must be enough equity to provide the investor with adequate security should the value of the property drop significantly.

There are lots of creative things you can do with private mortgages. But it's an active investment that requires you to do some things that you wouldn't be concerned with in a government-backed mortgage security. You have to record liens, collect checks, do tax reporting, and so on. You also have to be good at evaluating risk.

Private mortgages are often written between family members. This usually works to everyone's advantage. However, you do have to be concerned with what you, as the investor/lender, would do if your relatives default on their payments. Do you put up with it? Foreclose? This kind of thing can cause battles between family factions and may be more than you would want to deal with.

ALLOCATING RETIREMENT SAVINGS

The time-honored precepts of asset allocation, diversification, and a long time horizon remain worthy concepts for the risk-averse investor. The big difference between protected investment management and the traditional administration of investments is that common stocks and equity mutual funds are excluded from consideration because they can generate negative as well as positive returns.

Asset Allocation

The process of asset allocation helps the risk-averse investor to decide how to divide money between protected equities, fixed income, and cash. The traditional rule of thumb for asset allocation is that the percentage in equities should be 100 minus your age. For example, if you are 30 years old, 70 percent (100 – 30) should be in equities. If you are 65 years old, 35 percent should be in equities.

The selection of a particular allocation is as much an art as a science, but the general concept is that when we are young we seek potential growth of the principal and are able to incur higher risk, so more is allocated to the equity component. As we age and eventually need income from our investments, the allocation is shifted to bonds, other safe fixed income investments, and cash. There is no correct magic answer, but you will find lots of opinions on the subject. In an article written for *Newsweek* by financial columnist Jane Bryant Quinn, a section entitled "Roadmap for Retirement" suggests the 401(K) allocations shown on the next page.

Because of the many factors that come into determining asset allocation, this age-based chart is for illustration purposes only. I feel that this chart may be too aggressive in the earlier years and too conservative in the later years. Regardless of how the ultimate allocation is made, the protected investor will use market and equity-linked investments in place of stocks. Bonds will primarily be AAA rated and insured. Also, bond maturities will be laddered out over time to help deal with interest rate risk—the risk that future rates will be higher. When interest rates go up, it causes bonds to go down in value. If interest rate risk is properly dealt with, then low-

SAMPLE AGED-BASED
ASSET ALLOCATION[7]

AGE 26–45 **AGGRESSIVE**   100% IN STOCKS*
Now is time to be brave. Invest in higher-risk
stocks with greater growth potential.

AGE 45–55 **GROWTH**   90% IN STOCKS*
These are your peak earning   10% IN BONDS
years. Broadly diversify your portfolio.

AGE 55–65 **BALANCED**   60% IN STOCKS*
The house is paid off and kids are   30% IN BONDS
out of college; focus on higher   10% IN CASH
dividend yielding stocks.

AGE 65–75 **CONSERVATIVE**   10% IN STOCKS*
High dividend yielding equities such   70% IN BONDS
as utility stocks are the way to go.   20% IN CASH

AGE 76+ **SHORT-TERM**   0% IN STOCKS*
With no wages and a supersafe   10% IN BONDS
portfolio, your return starts   90% IN CASH
to suffer and your savings begin
to dwindle . . . but you should be OK
with what you have left.

---

* Risk-averse investors will use protected investments in lieu of stocks or mutual funds.

interest-earning cash equivalents such as money markets can be kept to a minimum.

Diversification

By using diversification we reduce risk. Too much money in one particular investment can be a recipe for disaster if that investment goes sour. The risk-averse investor, using only protected investments, can also benefit from diversification.

Once the proper asset allocation is decided upon, we then seek out the specific investments that are suitable for our retirement fund. For example, in the equity portion we will select from market-linked CDs and notes as well as equity-index annuities. Buying multiple CDs and notes based on different indexes and terms makes sense. The performance of even the most popular indexes can vary widely during certain periods. For example, there are times when larger companies like those found in the S&P 500 and Dow indexes will perform better than smaller companies represented in indexes such as the Russell 2000. Remember that the calculation of interest on some MCDs is based on a point-to-point method, while others are based on a quarterly average. Participation rates and caps will also vary between CD issues.

The policy date for an equity-index annuity with an annual reset is critical because this is the month and day used for determining the new beginning index for the following yearly period. If the starting indexes are low, there is a better chance of receiving an attractive interest return for the following year. Since we can't predict the future, it makes sense to diversify the policy dates and use different indexes and methodologies for calculating the interest. Once you have accumulated a reasonable amount with one insurance company, see if there are other insurance companies that offer a complementary equity-index annuity with different terms. For example, one company may offer a point-to-point interest methodology, while another uses a daily average. One method may be better than the other depending on how the market moves during the period.

Long-Term Time Horizon

If we didn't focus on the long term, we would only consider cash equivalents such as money market funds and short-term CDs as suitable investments. Having a long-term time horizon allows us to invest in three- to seven-year market-linked CDs and notes. As noted earlier, equity-index annuities have sur-render penalties and terms as long as fifteen years. For risk-averse investors, having a long-term outlook doesn't mean we buy into the concept that the market is *always* the best place to be and *always* comes through for us in the long run. It means that we believe the market will be volatile in the future and will have both bullish and bearish periods, and that we're sat-isfied with sharing in the gains of the up markets while avoid-ing the pain in the down markets.

AN ONGOING PHILOSOPHY

The market-linked investments used for our retirement accounts assure that our nest eggs will remain intact while still allowing us to participate safely in stock market gains. These products fit an overall philosophy of personal risk management that keeps us in control of the principal value of our invest-ments. If we lose command of our principal, the attainment of our financial goals becomes dependent upon factors beyond our control. We become gamblers with our savings, and as we've seen earlier in this chapter as well as in Chapters 1 and 2, most of us are likely to make poor decisions that reduce our potential returns, even during the good times.

If we maintain an ongoing regimen of keeping our personal expenses under control relative to our income and use the dif-ference to pay down high-interest debt first and then consider protected investments within our retirement savings, we have a good shot at reaching our long-term goals. These goals com-monly include *financial independence*—the ability to retire without having to worry about money.

We have to stay focused on our strict definition of risk and not be taken in by the many investments that are advertised as safe or conservative without proper due diligence of the true risk. For example, a $100,000 thirty-year zero coupon govern-ment bond, purchased to yield 5 percent, will cost approximately $23,100. If interest rates jump to 7 percent, the bond will be worth only $13,100, a drop of 43 percent. An advertisement for this bond may focus on the fact that this is a AAA rated government bond. The credit risk is small, but the interest rate risk in this type of investment is huge.

■ ■ ■

How you plan for retirement and choose the appropriate retirement investments can result in tremendously different lifestyles after leaving the workforce. Unless there are radical changes in the way we save and invest, as many as 20 percent of retiring baby boomers will be living in abject poverty, completely dependent on government assistance. Studies show that only half of the workers between ages 47 and 64 plan to be collecting even 50 percent of their current income at retirement. Many will have far less.

CHAPTER ELEVEN

REFORMING THE SYSTEM

*Creative thinking may simply mean the realization
that there is no particular virtue in doing things
the way they have always been done.*

RUDOLPH FLESCH, PHILOSOPHER AND EDUCATOR,
WWW.LINEZINE.COM

OVERHAUL!

WE HAVE SEEN the tremendous conflicts of interest that plague corporations and their CEOs, the accounting industry, the brokerage industry, and even our federal government. These conflicts contributed to the shocking evaporation of wealth that investors endured in the early 2000s when the market bubble finally burst.

The solution to these problems isn't easy. It will take a concerted effort by all concerned to re-create a fair and equitable capital system in which the investor gets a reasonable return that is proportionate to the risk assumed when purchasing equities. The markets will eventually provide such a solution, either through decreased share prices or meaningful change at all levels. If reformation doesn't occur, further harm to stock portfolios is inevitable.

Investors who employ strategies for protecting principal are prepared for any scenario. The major overhaul required to win back investor faith and confidence is a huge and complex undertaking. Conflicts of interest still exist, which make the task a strenuous challenge.

A Taxing Situation

The American public is entitled to be fed up with corporations as well as the regulators, analysts, and auditors who are expected to assure that this system that spawns greed and arrogance doesn't get too far out of control. Situations that would have seemed impossible, surreal, and undemocratic 200 years ago are part of everyday life today. We need to rekindle the revolutionary spirit of yesteryear and break out of this downward spiral of economic servitude.

Our capital system should be based on fairness among all participants in the economy. Shareholders, employees, and ordinary citizens of the United States are being taken advantage of by corporations and, in a sense, their own government, whose policies enable the continuation of the current system that creates wealth for the benefit of the few.

Just reflect on our tax code and the many ways corporations reduce their tax burden. When companies employ strategies to reduce the taxes they would otherwise be paying, it puts the burden back on individuals to pick up the tab.

Consider the research of finance professors Simon Pak, of Pennsylvania State University, and John Zdanowicz, from my alma mater, Florida International University, on corporate tax evasion from international trade transactions. Cheating Uncle Sam is a relatively simple process for the multinational corporation. For example, a Japanese automaker manufactures a car radio for $100, but its U.S. subsidiary buys it for $199, then sells it for $200. The company's bottom line hasn't changed, but the taxable profit in the United States is now just $1 instead of $100. A tax bill that would have been $34 is reduced to 34 cents. This is why U.S. companies are paying as much as $113 a piece for imported razor blades from Britain and $4,896 for tweezers from Japan.

The converse is true as well, as U.S. trading partners get the deals of a century: car seats exported to Belgium for $1.66 each, missile launchers to Israel for $52 a shot, and watches encased in precious metals to Colombia for $8.68 a pop. There is no profit recognized at these prices in the United States, but the profit is recognized overseas, where the tax rates are lower or nonexistent. Pak and Zdanowicz calculate that this transfer pricing cost the public treasury $53 billion in 2001 alone![2]

The Tax Reform Act of 1986 was passed to deal with the abusive tax shelters that resulted from the passage of the Economic Recovery Tax Act of 1981. Investors were able to write off far more than their investment in real estate and real estate partnerships and, as a result, greatly reduce or even eliminate their tax liability. Real estate was being developed and deals being struck not from need but purely because of the tax benefits. The 1986 act pulled the rug out from under this game and caused a temporary collapse in commercial real estate prices that ultimately led to the downfall of virtually the entire savings and loan industry, which eagerly provided the financing for these ventures.

Individuals and small closely held corporations now have to abide by the "passive loss" rule, which strictly limits the amount that an investor can deduct from real estate investment losses primarily caused by depreciation. However, large corporations were exempted from the passive loss rule. Large corporations can use passive losses to offset any amount of income from any source even to the point of bringing taxes down to zero. With the financial lifeline of both major political parties connected so tightly to corporate interests, it shouldn't be surprising that the tax code closes an abusive loophole to individuals but lets large corporations continue to use this tax dodge freely and legally.

CORPORATIONS AND THEIR EXECUTIVES

I worked for several large profitable corporations early in my career. I always shook my head in wonder at the chaos and how some of these organizations could be showing positive earnings. It always seemed as if very few people, including those at the top, had an adequate handle on the big picture. The politics, the meetings, the absolutely stupid decisions—it was maddening!

The total compensation of some of these so-called executives at the top seemed totally out of line with reality. Some were earning the equivalent of what 400 to 500 employees earned. The situation has gotten even worse over time. Today, I equate some of these executive compensation packages to legalized theft from shareholders. Stock option incentive plans can enrich management beyond comprehension and certainly way beyond their contribution to the success of the business.

In addition, the accounting for stock option compensation makes no sense. If it's compensation and acting as a drag on shareholders, it's only logical that it should be treated as an expense. But we need to do more than accounting reform. We need to go back to the original argument against the legality of options and consider them for what they really are—corporate waste. The stock option as a compensation tool should be completely eliminated. Stock options help to drive management's focus on the short-term performance of the stock's price. This in turn creates a conflict of interest between the long-term owners of the company (the shareholders) and management. Executives come and go, but while they are at the helm, many definitely try to make the most of it for *themselves.*

It is fair for management to receive higher compensation than other employees because they have more responsibility. But shareholders should demand that top management receive maximum compensation based on a multiple of the firm's lowest-paid employees. For example, if the multiple is 60 and the lowest-paid employee makes $20,000 per year, top management shouldn't make more than $1.2 million. This multiple could be adjusted up and down based on the size and nature of the firm.

■ ■ ■

The straightforward task of corporate accounting has become a convoluted mess. Generally Accepted Accounting Principles (GAAP) allow too much leeway and judgment on the part of corporate management. There are some simple ways to solve this problem and force proper accounting.

Reporting Assets

Corporations should only report assets that have a tangible value on their balance sheets, and these values should be based on what the asset is actually worth. Just study a corporation's balance sheet and the amounts it lists as assets. Some companies have *billions* of dollars of intangible assets such as goodwill. These "assets" have zero value. The company can't sell or redeem them for cash and never expects to realize anything from them, yet they are still listed as assets.

If a corporation reports only its tangible net worth to its shareholders, it becomes much harder to cook the books and play with the numbers. It's also much easier for outside auditors to concentrate on the verification of asset values instead of tiptoeing around this issue. If the tangible net worth of a firm has increased over the period, a profit has been made. If it has decreased, there was a loss. If a company makes a boneheaded acquisition and pays over $40 billion for another company with assets of half a billion dollars, as JDS Uniphase did in its purchase of SDL, Inc. in early 2001, the difference of over $39.5 billion should be reported as an immediate loss after the purchase.

Management should have to answer to shareholders as to why they think it's good for the company to pay out a dollar and receive less than two cents of assets in return. That $39.5 billion was booked as goodwill and appeared as a "phantom" asset on the company's books shortly after the acquisition.

The common practice of pro forma accounting and reporting earnings before income taxes, depreciation, and amortization (EBITDA) should be prohibited. It's fine if a company wants to include this as supplementary information, but these numbers should not be referred to in a press release.

Reporting Liabilities

Corporations need to report all of their liabilities. Innovative accountants have masterminded methods for hiding liabilities by using vehicles such as offshore subsidiaries.

A firm's pension liabilities and assets should be clearly stated on the net worth statement. Nowadays you have to scour the footnotes to the financial statements to find these important details. In addition, the actual value of the pension liabilities should always be reported instead of some fictitious number based on an unrealistic assumed interest rate as is commonly done today. Companies should all be required to use a uniform interest rate such as the rate on thirty-year treasury bonds.

ACCOUNTANTS AND REGULATORS

Accounting for the large corporation is an exceedingly complex task. A company like Citigroup has subsidiaries in over 100 different countries. Many of these countries have accounting standards that differ from those used in the United States. There are at least twenty-six different methods of accounting used throughout the world that affect U.S. corporations. Consolidating all of this into one statement is a herculean task.[3]

Generally, accountants do the best they can to present an accurate picture of a company's financial posture. Unfortunately, there are far too many areas in which judgment plays a part in determining how and when to report certain items. Accountants are conservative by nature, but they come under immense pressure from upper management to portray the numbers in a positive light. As a former accountant, I remember the pressure to get creative and make the numbers look better so that my firm's management would make or come close to its projections.

The Securities and Exchange Commission tries to assure that there is a level playing field by requiring corporations to make full disclosures, but they can't force investors to read them or prevent investors from making foolish mistakes.

Back in the 1980s a couple of hucksters scammed a group of investors out of $120 million. Amazingly they carefully laid out their scheme in the prospectus they gave to potential investors. They disclosed the huge fees they took out of the deal and the fact that the business had virtually no chance of being profitable. At the same time, they projected a 17 percent tax-free return, and the investors bought into it without looking at the details. Very few investors bother looking at financial statements or disclosures. And the sad fact is that very few investment professionals bother looking at them either.[4]

It's our responsibility to read the fine print and understand what we choose to invest in. If there is a guarantee against loss, it's essential to know when and how we collect on the promise. Plenty of bad investments can easily be avoided if we take the time to understand the risks and properly evaluate the potential for rewards.

Taking Advantage of Investors

I received an unsolicited email from something called the OTC Newsletter, "Discover Tomorrow's Winners," in August 2002. It touted a stock by saying a "licensed and registered investment expert" says now is the time to buy it. There were lots of reasons to buy, according to the email. They are reproduced verbatim here:

1. Liquidity will increase including coverage by other analysts

2. *Has a network of strategic alliances designed to assist company in obtaining DOMINANT MARKET SHARE*

3. *Current market in which company operates is expected to grow between $900 million and $25 billion*

4. *Company growing at fast rate*

5. *One of the fastest growing companies in its field*

6. *Company is profitable and on track to beat all earnings estimates*

7. *Impressive client list including Chevron, GE, and the U.S. Air Force*

8. *Buy now. Price will hit $2 in 4 months and $5 in 16 months.*

Just for fun I looked up the stock and actually found a financial statement filed with the SEC. The company was a sole proprietorship and had divided itself into three impressive sounding divisions. That one employee must be pretty busy!

The company had $1,400 in cash, $4,000 worth of furniture, and a $2,400 deposit on the office that it leases. That about sums it up. The liabilities exceeded assets, resulting in a negative net worth of $8,200. The company had six-month revenues of $138,000 and six months of expenses of $140,000. Most of the expenses were related to the salary of the sole employee.

It looks like the one employee is some sort of manufacturer's sales rep who gets paid a commission. This employee decided to incorporate but is making sure that he takes out everything that he makes in salary. Of course the one employee is president and chairman and has grand plans for this business in the future. According to SEC filings, the "insiders" are selling from $50,000 to $100,000 of this company's stock each month.

Here is a guy who has been grossing about $200,000 a year in commissions from selling who knows what. The SEC filing says phonograph records. He incorporates. He buys a shell of a company for virtually nothing, and that company purchases his business for stock and starts pumping the stock. At a minimum he pays a stock promoter (most likely with stock) to blast emails to investors around the country. Enough interest is generated each month to allow him to sell miniscule pieces of his worthless company to investors so that he makes an additional $600,000 to over $1 million each year. What a scam!

Believe it or not, there are over 21 million shares outstanding, and the stock trades for 40 cents a share. This means that the market values this fledgling company at over $8 million! This person has discovered the real secret of making money in the market with little risk: *taking advantage of investors.*

Would it surprise you to know that there are many similar companies doing this? It's certainly unethical but in most cases perfectly legal. Regulators have no power to crack down on these kinds of operations except to require disclosure. But obviously the disclosures are not read or comprehended by investors.

Many investors don't understand what they are actually purchasing when they make an investment. If everyone truly understood the real risks of gambling on stocks, there would be far fewer people willing to place their hard-earned dollars on the line.

THE BROKERAGE INDUSTRY

In early 2002, a court order by the New York attorney general described the purpose of a major brokerage firm's research department as "attracting and keeping investment banking clients, thereby producing misleading ratings that were neither objective nor independent, as they purported to be."[5]

Investment banking firms should be prohibited from publishing research on any company. The average investor thinks there is value in the firm's recommendations when in reality the suggestions are virtually useless.

Investors would be better off avoiding investment research reports when they are making an investment decision. This applies to ongoing buy, hold, and sell recommendations from the firm's analysts.

■ ■ ■

The hundreds of new mutual funds that are churned out each year by the investment industry are not helping investors. The thousands of managers and advisers who promise market-beating returns are ignoring history and the fact that it's impossible to provide consistent superior returns without taking on added risk. The time spent and fees charged for these services are a waste of resources.

The average investor would be best served if the industry provided more authentic ways to eliminate or reduce the threat of loss to an individual's money beyond the tired method of investing in stock and utilizing asset allocation, diversification, and a long-term time horizon to address market risk.

Market-linked and guaranteed products give the investor the potential for above-average returns while controlling the danger that is usually inherent in seeking higher returns. Investment advisers are in a unique position to give advice relating to such risk-management decisions by investors. But the advisers themselves need to rethink the arcane teachings of wealth management that have been drummed into their heads.

If investment advisers did nothing else but observe the behavior of their clients, they would perceive that what clients really want is not to lose money. When the overall market is up

15 percent and an individual's investment is up 10 percent, the investor is usually happy, even though the objective of beating the market was a miserable failure. Now if the market is down 15 percent and the investor is down 10 percent, the investor is not at all happy, even though the performance was better than the overall market.

To thrive in the future, the investment industry needs to provide more education, products, and services that are desperately wanted and needed by the average investor. To continue the pattern of pushing the same old stuff down the average investor's throat will eventually result in an upheaval of dissent and disgust. The author of an article in our local small newspaper, the *Medford Mail Tribune*, expressed this growing anger as follows:

I have saved myself broke with automatic transfers from my paycheck to my 401(K) . . . I have watched the bottom line sink lower with every statement—even as I was putting money in. I feel as though I have been transfusing a patient through one artery while he bleeds to death through another.

Well no more. I have pulled the plug on these investments in my future.

How stupid do I look Merrill Lynch? What kind of chump do you take me for Fidelity? Do you think I was going to keep giving you money so you could blow it?

I feel as if I have a brother with a big time gambling problem. Well you are cut off. . . . You have stolen my future. What a scam! Instead of funding retirement for their workers, the workers are funding the stock options, golden parachutes and defense attorney fees of their employers.

Meanwhile across town the boys at Merrill Lynch, Fidelity and the like were talking us into buying crummy stocks that were only good for commissions and bonuses. We were literally paying for bad advice! Fool me once shame on me. But you won't fool me twice.[6]

THE INDIVIDUAL INVESTOR

The unprotected investor is always at the mercy of the whimsical changes that occur in the marketplace. This fact is conveniently forgotten during roaring bull markets and painfully remembered in tumbling bear markets.

The economy, corporate behavior, investment company actions, and the stock market are out of our immediate control. Cross your fingers and pray that the market goes up because our savings, children's education funds, retirement funds—our very lives—have been tied to the markets. But we can choose not to subject our portfolio and ourselves to such agonizing volatility and to regain control of our financial destiny.

We have the economic freedom and the power not to participate in the skullduggery of unprotected investments in the stock market. Our economic system is in serious need of an overhaul, but the beneficiaries of the current system have too much at stake to make any meaningful changes. There have been some cosmetic reforms, but we need much more. If we pull our money off the gambling table and refuse to place our bets, we could see positive change take place from business itself. Government regulations can help, but stockholders and consumers have ultimate control of the lifeblood of the corporation—money.

These changes would hopefully include a resurgence of small business, in which investor control is clearly defined, and a decrease in the power of big business, whose structure creates many problems, ranging from societal concerns to unethical activity that hurts the owner-shareholders. We'll also see more investment possibilities to choose from that meet *Webster's* definition of an investment, not *Wall Street's*.

We need to realize that stock investing, when mixed with human emotion, is not a formula for success. We have to distance ourselves from market timing decisions and investments that can implode without warning. We should never put ourselves in a position where we have to agonize over whether to buy or sell a security, because we'll usually make the wrong decision.

We need to put pressure on our employers to offer protected investment alternatives for 401(K) and other retirement plans instead of just more mutual fund choices. Protected investment alternatives are available *today.* Self-directed 401(K) plans can be designed to give the risk-averse investor attractive investment choices. It won't happen unless we tell our employers that we want some intelligent options for our retirement accounts, not just more mutual funds.

We hold the keys to creating positive individual and societal change by removing our support of what some would argue is a corrupt system. The scheme depends upon the willingness of the individual investor to continue to fuel this out-of-control train by shoveling money into individual stock and mutual equity funds. Pull out of these investments and you regain personal control of your money and are no longer a passenger on this wild ride that determines your financial future.

America was born of a revolution against the abusive power exercised by the British monarchy in the 1700s. The crown controlled the colonies through chartered corporations such as the East India Company, the Hudson's Bay Company, and the Royal Africa Company. These corporations exercised total authority over the colonists—conscripting them into corporate militia, instructing them on what to grow, what work to do, where to buy goods, and where to market their products.

It is our economic freedom that allows us to rebel against the new kind of dominance corporations and their leaders brazenly employ to take advantage of American citizens over 200 years after the signing of the Declaration of Independence. The power we can demonstrate simply by changing our investment and spending habits can totally improve not just our own personal finances but also the course of human history.

We can avoid the prophecy of President Abraham Lincoln, who said just before his death:

> *I see in the future a crisis approaching that unnerves me and causes me to tremble for the safety of my country. . . . Corporations have been enthroned, an era of corruption in high places will follow and the money power of the country will endeavor to prolong its reign by working on the prejudices of the people until the wealth is aggregated in a few hands and the Republic is destroyed.*[7]

Let us reclaim our destiny and keep it in our own hands, where it belongs!

USING OPTIONS TO REDUCE RISK

Options are derivative contracts that have no value on their own. They derive their worth from the value of some other asset. They are used to reduce risk and are the most sophisticated, intricate, and arcane of the financial instruments.

If used improperly, options can be among the riskiest of investments. In the early 1990s some institutions that obviously lacked a full understanding of the risks and consequences of the inappropriate application of derivatives became high-profile casualties of improper usage. An electric saw can be a valuable tool in skilled hands or a dangerous one in the hands of a careless individual. Orange County lost an estimated $2 billion and Long Term Capital, $4 billion from the bungled use of derivatives. The accompanying negative publicity gave these tools of risk management a tainted reputation.[1]

UNDERSTANDING PUTS AND CALLS

The *call option* is an agreement that gives the investor the right but not the obligation to purchase a security at a specified price within a specified period of time. Conversely, a *put option* gives the investor the right to sell a security at a specified price for a specified time.

You can buy or sell both put and call options. These kinds of instruments can make your head spin because of the many possible variations and combinations of option contracts. There are some simple and conservative ways to use puts and calls. Some of these strategies are as follows:

- Sell covered calls
- Purchase a protective put
- Sell uncovered puts
- Purchase calls

Sell Covered Calls

Let's say Karen owns 1,000 shares of Intel, which is currently trading at $28 per share. She would be absolutely thrilled if it went to $35 in the next five months. This would amount to a 25 percent increase. As a matter of fact, she is willing to give someone else the right to buy her stock between now and five months from now at $35. She'll give away all appreciation above $35 to the other party. For giving this up she receives an immediate payment called an *option premium.* Let's assume she will receive $1,250, or $1.25 per share. She keeps this money regardless of what happens with the stock price. If Intel is above $35 in five months, it will be sold at $35. If it's below $35, she keeps the stock (as well as the option premium) and can write another round of covered calls if she wishes. This is a conservative strategy for stock investors and is called *covered call writing.*

What if she sold the call options but didn't own the underlying stock in Intel? This is a very high-risk strategy. She would receive the $1.25 per share option premium, but her losses are theoretically unlimited. Let's say she does this and Intel is at $60 five months from now. She has the obligation to deliver Intel stock at a price of $35 per share. She received $1,250 from the option premium but lost $25,000 by having to buy Intel at its current price of $60 to cover the shares that were sold for $35. Obviously, the conservative investor would consider this an unreasonable strategy.

Purchase a Protective Put

Let's assume that Karen still owns Intel, and it is at $28 per share. She is worried about the economy. Some economists are forecasting robust results, while others see a severe recession. She feels that Intel will do well in a rebound and could even double in price in the next year. But if the economy falters, she fears that Intel could go all the way down to $10 per share. She wouldn't want to suffer that kind of drop.

She is willing to pay $3 per share, or $3,000, if someone else guarantees that he will purchase her Intel shares at $25 for the next twelve months, if she wants to sell. Of course, she would only do this if the share price was less than $25 at the end of the twelve months. Let's say Intel goes down to $10 per share. She exercises her options to sell at $25. Karen nets $25 less the option premium of $3, or $22 per share. She still lost money, but $22,000 is better than $10,000. Essentially, she bought portfolio insurance with a deductible. The higher the deductible (losses you are willing to absorb), the lower the premium. Now if the stock doubled to $56 per share, her account would be valued at $53,000 ($56 – $3 option premium). The put option gives you a predetermined maximum loss and unlimited gains.

If you don't own Intel and just buy a put option, you are speculating that the price will come down. If it doesn't come down, you lose 100 percent of your investment. The loss in this case is limited to the amount of your investment.

Sell Uncovered Puts

Now let's say that Karen doesn't own Intel, and it is currently at $28. This is a stock she would like to purchase, but only if it gets down to $25 per share. She could put a buy limit order in at $25, meaning that if Intel were to go down to $25, her order to purchase 1,000 shares would go through at that price. Instead she sells put options on Intel that obligate her to purchase at $25 if it is at or below that price twelve months from now. She immediately receives an option premium of $3 per share for taking on this obligation. She keeps this regardless of what happens to the stock price of Intel. If the option is exercised, she buys at $25 per share, but she received $3 for the option premium so her net investment is really $22. If the stock price stays above $25, she won't get to buy Intel but keeps the $3,000 option premium.

You can see that this could be a risky strategy because if the stock goes down a lot, you are on the hook for buying at the exercise price. In the event the stock price goes to zero, your maximum loss is the cost of the stock at exercise, less the option premium.

Purchase Calls

Karen thinks Intel is going to soar but doesn't want to sink $28,000 into the stock in case she is wrong. She buys ten call option contracts (each contract represents 100 shares of stock) that give her the right to purchase Intel at $35 per share for a five-month period. The cost is $1,250. By purchasing the option she is limiting her maximum loss to the option premium. So if Intel goes down to $5 or $10 per share, her loss is $1,250 and no more. She simply chooses not to exercise the option. However, if Intel gets to $56, she would exercise her option to purchase at $35 and have a gain of $21,000 less the $1,250 cost of the contracts, or $19,750. She could also sell her option before it expires and make a profit. You can see that there is huge leverage here if the stock goes up, while the downside is limited to the amount invested.

All of this may sound very complicated, but many people are unsuspecting buyers of options. Anyone who has ever purchased a home and taken out a mortgage with a no-penalty prepayment provision actually owns an option. In this case the homeowner-borrower has the option to determine the conditions of repayment. If mortgage rates drop, the homeowner can refinance and take out a mortgage with a lower rate of interest, leaving the lender with a loss of a high-interest loan replaced by a low-interest loan. This option is pretty much standard with most loans today. The borrower is actually paying for this option by paying a slightly higher interest rate for the no-prepayment provision clause.

Options can be a useful device for protecting the value of a stock portfolio from devastating losses. However, the investor should be cautious and work with a financial professional who thoroughly understands all the intricacies of how they function.

CREDIT RATINGS

Credit ratings assist in evaluating the level of credit risk involved when investing in equity-linked notes, annuities, and insurance. Each rating organization uses a slightly different system. The highest four ratings encompass what is referred to as "investment grade bonds." All ratings below the four highest are in the "junk" category. Moody's and Standard & Poor's publicize ratings on corporations and each has its own unique grading system.

S&P	MOODY'S	RISK
AAA	Aaa	The absolute highest quality
AA	Aa	High quality by all standards
A	A	Upper medium grade
BBB	Baa	Medium grade
BB	Ba	Lower grade, speculative elements
B	B	Lack characteristics of desirable investment
CCC	Caa	Poor standing; in default or close to it
CC	Ca	Speculative to high degree; in default or close to it
C	C	Poor prospects of ever getting better, no matter what
D		The worst of the worst

As of the date of this writing, the more frequent issuers of equity-linked notes had investment grade ratings as follows:

COMPANY	S&P RATING	MOODY'S RATING
Bear Stearns	A	A2
Goldman Sachs	A+	A1
JPMorgan Chase	AA–	Aa3
Lehman Brothers	A	A2
Merrill Lynch	AA–	Aa3
Salomon Smith Barney	AA–	Aa1

Additional modifiers indicate whether the rating is at the top, middle, or bottom for each category. S&P uses plusses and minuses, and Moody's uses 1, 2, 3, with 1 being the highest. *Source:* Moodys.com and Bloomberg Financial.

Ratings are fluid and can be changed at any time by the rating companies. Insurance companies have their own unique ratings. A. M. Best ratings are as follows:

A++ and A+   Superior
A and A-   Excellent
B++ and B+   Very good[1]

Anything below a B+ should not even be considered. A. M. Best rates the leading companies that offer equity-index annuities as Superior. Weiss Ratings uses a different methodology for measuring the financial strength of insurance companies. The ratings are as follows:

A   Excellent
B   Good
C   Fair
D   Weak
E   Very Weak

If a company has a Weiss rating of C or below, it should be eliminated from consideration.

NOTES

CHAPTER 1—THE STOCK MARKET:
CAN WE WIN AT THIS GAME?

1. "Quantitative Analysis of Investor Behavior," www.dalbarinc. com, June 21, 2001.

2. Jason Zweig, "What Fund Investors Really Need to Know," *Money* 31 (June 2002): 110–115.

3. "Retirement out of Reach," Economic Policy Institute Briefing Paper, August 2002.

4. "Massively Confused Investors Making Conspicuously Ignorant Choices," *Journal of Finance* (October 2001).

5. Burton G. Malkiel, *A Random Walk down Wall Street* (New York: W. W. Norton, 1985).

6. Charles Ellis, *Winning the Losers Game* (New York: McGraw-Hill, 1998), 5.

7. Max Isaacman, *How to Be an Index Investor* (New York: McGraw-Hill, 2000).

8. Jonathan Clements, "Stock Funds Just Don't Measure Up," *Wall Street Journal,* 5 October 1999, C1.

9. Jonathan Clements, "Not Everyone Can Pick Funds. Really," *Wall Street Journal,* 9 November 1999, C1.

10. Peter L. Bernstein, "Where Oh Where Are the .400 Hitters of Yesteryear?" *The Financial Analysts' Journal* 54 (November-December 1998): 6–14.

11. "Performance Evaluation with Transactions Data: The Stock Selection of Investment Newsletters," *Journal of Finance* (October 1999): 1743–1775.

12. "A Step Beyond Index Funds," *Investment Advisor* (November 2000): 151.

13. Elroy Dimson and Paul Marsh, *Millennium Book II: 101 Years of Investment Returns* (Princeton: Princeton University Press, 2001).

14. Michael Sivy, *Michael Sivy's Rules of Investing* (New York: Warner Books, 1996).

15. Jane Bryant Quinn, *Making the Most of Your Money* (New York: Simon & Schuster, 1997).

16. Edward Jones, "What to Do When Bad News Hits Your Stocks," *Women in Business* 53 (May/June 2001).

17. Remarks by Chairman Arthur Levitt, Securities and Exchange Commission, at NYU Center for Law and Business, New York, September 28, 1998.

18. "Enron Analysts Eerily Saw Phantom Profits," *Investment News* (February 25, 2002).

19. Ben Shouse, "The Power of Napping," *ScienceNOW* (May 29, 2002):14.

20. "The Psychology of Investing," *Focus Gold* (February 2000).

**CHAPTER 2—FAITH IN OURSELVES:
THE IRRATIONAL BEHAVIOR OF INVESTORS**

1. "The Dutch Triangle: A Framework to Measure Upside Potential Relative to Downside Risk," *Journal of Portfolio Management* (Fall 1999): 50.

2. "Cognitive Biases in Market Forecasts—The Frailty of Forecasting," *Journal of Portfolio Management* (Fall 2000): 72.

3. Bridget O'Brian, "When It Hurts Too Much to Look," *Wall Street Journal,* 11 October 2002, C1.

4. Daniel Kahneman and Amos Tversky, "On the Psychology of Prediction," *Psychological Review* 80 (July 1973): 251.

5. Peter Bernstein, *Against the Gods: The Remarkable Story of Risk* (New York: John Wiley & Sons, 1996).

6. Hillel J. Einhorn and Robin M. Hogarth, "Confidence in Judgment: Persistence of the Illusion of Validity," *Psychological Review* 85 (September 1978): 395.

7. William J. Broad, "Data Tying Cancer to Electrical Power Found to be False," *New York Times,* 24 July 1999, A1.

8. Terrance Odean, "Do Investors Trade Too Much?" *American Economic Review* 89 (December 1999): 1279.

9. Daniel Kadlec, "Day Trading: It's a Brutal World," *Time* 154 (August 9, 1999).

10. William O'Barr and John Conley, *Fortune and Folly: The Wealth and Power of Institutional Investing* (Chicago: Irwin Professional Publications, 1992).

11. Tom Lahman, "Why You Should Offer Investment Counseling," *ABA Banking Journal* 89 (June 1997): 61.

12. "Psychology and Behavioral Finance," www.investorhome.com/psych.htm.

13. Robert J. Shiller, *Irrational Exuberance* (Princeton: Princeton University Press, 2000).

14. John Ellis, "Q: What Is the New Economics?" *Fast Company* (September 2001): 118.

15. Gustave Le Bon, *The Crowd: A Study of the Popular Mind* (Mineola, NY: Dover Publications, 2002).

16. Richard Swift interviews Stuart Ewen, "One Trick Pony," *New Internationalist* (July 1999): 16.

17. Charles Mackay, *Memoirs of Extraordinary Popular Delusions and the Madness of Crowds* (1841; New York: Farrar Straus and Giroux, 1974).

18. John Kenneth Galbraith, *A Short History of Financial Euphoria* (New York: Penguin, 1993).

19. Timothy L. O'Brien, *Bad Bet: The Inside Story of the Glamour, Glitz, and Danger in America's Gambling Industry* (New York: NY Times Books, 1998).

20. Sally Denton, "Big Deal in Vegas," *Columbia Journalism Review* 39 (Nov/Dec 2000): 46.

21. Victor A. Matheson, "When Are State Lotteries a Good Bet (Revisited)?" *Eastern Economic Journal* 27 (Winter 2001): 55.

22. "Look Out, Vegas," *The Economist* 356 (July 15, 2000): 30.

23. Robert Goodman, *The Luck Business: The Devastating Consequences and Broken Promises of America's Gambling Explosion* (New York: The Free Press, 1995).

24. Adam Smith, *An Inquiry into the Nature and Causes of the Wealth of Nations* (1776; New York: Modern Library, 1937).

25. Jane Bryant Quinn, *Making the Most of Your Money* (New York: Simon & Schuster, 1997), 600–602.

26. Suze Orman, *The 9 Steps to Financial Freedom* (New York: Random House, 1997), 222.

CHAPTER 3—FAITH IN CORPORATIONS: TRICKS OF THE TRADE

1. "Accounting for Option Based Compensation," *E-Commerce Tax News,* November 12, 2000.

2. Gretchen Morgenson, "Stock Options Are Not a Free Lunch," *Forbes* 161 (May 18, 1998).

3. "Employee Stock Option Accounting Implications," press release, Parish & Company, September 30, 1998.

4. Morgenson, "Stock Options Are Not a Free Lunch."

5. David Henry, "The Numbers Game—Companies Use Every Trick to Pump Earnings and Fool Investors," *Business Week* (May 14, 2001): 103.

6. Henry, "The Numbers Game," 104.

7. Matthew Swibel, "Dial 'D' for Dummies," *Forbes* 169 (March 18, 2002).

8. Henry, "The Numbers Game."

9. "Blockbuster Takes $450 Million Write-off," press release, Blockbuster Inc., September 10, 2001.

10. "Blockbuster Reports Strong Cash Earnings," press release: Blockbuster Inc., July 24, 2001.

11. Lou Dobbs, "Toothless Tigers," *Money* 31 (September 2002): 63.

12. Miles Maguire, "Business as Usual," *American Journalism Review* 24 (October 2002): 18.

CHAPTER 4—FAITH IN PROFESSIONAL ADVICE: CONFLICTS OF INTEREST

1. Peter Elkind, "Where Mary Meeker Went Wrong," *Fortune* 143 (May 14, 2001): 76.

2. Elkind, "Where Mary Meeker Went Wrong," 78.

3. Bethany McLean, "Hear No Risk, See No Risk, Speak No Risk," *Fortune* 143 (May 14, 2001).

4. David Dreman, "Fantasy Earnings," *Forbes* 168 (October 1, 2001): 134.

5. "With Analysts, You Get What You Pay For," *New York Times,* 7 September 2001.

6. Amy Feldman, "Sue Your Broker," *Money* 30 (October 2001): 102.

7. Andy Serwer, "Wall Street Story," *Fortune* 146 (July 28, 2002).

8. Alan Abelson, "Fun & Games," *Barron's* (November 12, 2001).

9. Securities & Exchange Commission, JDS Uniphase 10-Q filing, June 30, 2000.

10. Justin Wiser, "Earnings Are so Passé," *Kiplinger's Personal Finance* 55 (January 2001).

11. Andy Reinhardt, "Is JDS Uniphase Bonkers?" *Business Week* (July 24, 2000): 33.

12. Donald Coxe, "Innovative Accounting," *Macleans* 114, (August 20, 2001): 35.

13. Louis Lavelle, "Executive Pay," *Business Week* (April 16, 2001).

14. *Canadian Business* (April 16, 2001): 24.

15. "How High Is Up?" *Canadian Business* 72 (December 10, 1999): 24.

CHAPTER 5—THE REAL WINNERS
OF THE STOCK MARKET GAME

1. Institute for Policy Studies and United for a Fair Economy, "The 1990s: A Decade of Greed," Eighth Annual Report on Executive Excess, August 28, 2001.

2. "A Corporate Bailout at Workers Expense," *Los Angeles Times,* November 2001.

3. Executive Pay Watch 2000, www.aflcio.org.

4. Geoffrey Colvin, "The Great CEO Pay Heist," *Fortune* 143 (June 25, 2001).

5. Remarks by retired Chairman Laura S. Unger, June 25, 2001, www.sec.gov.

6. "Runaway CEO Pay: What's Happening and What You Can Do about It," www.aflcio.org, 2000.

7. Louis Lavelle, "Executive Pay," *Business Week* (April 16, 2001): 79.

8. Mark Gimein, "You Bought, They Sold," *Fortune* 146 (September 2, 2002).

9. Christopher Palmeri and Steven Brull, "If You've Got It, Spend It," *Business Week* (October 16, 2000).

10. Eric L. Johnson, "Waste Not, Want Not: An Analysis of Stock Option Plans, Executive Compensation, and the Proper Standard of Waste," *Journal of Corporation Law* 26 (Fall 2000): 145.

11. Steve Cocheo, "Pooling's Demise Is Not Mourned," *ABA Banking Journal* 94 (April 2002).

12. "AOL and Time Warner Will Merge to Create World's First Internet-Age Media & Communications Company," press release, AOL, Time Warner, January 10, 2000.

13. Shawn Tully, "Betrayal on Wall Street," *Fortune* 143 (May 14, 2001): 86.

14. Tully, "Betrayal on Wall Street."

15. Adam Smith, *An Inquiry into the Nature and Causes of the Wealth of Nations* (1776; New York: Modern Library, 1937), 60–61.

CHAPTER 6—RISK MANAGEMENT

1. Gary Brinson, Randolph Hood, and Gilbert Beebower, "Determinants of Portfolio Performance," *The Financial Analysts' Journal* (July/August 1986): 39.

2. Harry M. Markowitz, *Portfolio Selection and Efficient Diversification of Investments* (New York: John Wiley & Sons, 1967).

3. Robert Esperiti and Renno Peterson, *21st Century Wealth, Essential Financial Planning Principles* (Denver: Quantum Press, 2000), 73.

4. *The New McClures,* August 1928, author's personal copy.

CHAPTER 7—MAINTAINING CONTROL OF OUR FINANCIAL FUTURE

1. "Social Problems on Rise, U.S. Health Check Shows," *Seattle Post-Intelligencer,* 14 January 1992.

2. Betsy Morris, "Big Spenders: As a Favored Pastime Shopping Ranks High with Most Americans," *Wall Street Journal,* 30 July 1987.

3. Lawrence Shames, *The Hunger for More* (New York: NY Times Books, 1991), 43.

4. "Would You Believe These Are the Good Old Days," *Seattle Times,* 19 September 1993.

CHAPTER 8—THE MATCHING GAME: INVESTING IN THE INDEXES

1. Mindy Charski, "Following the Gospel of Indexing's St. Jack," *U.S. News & World Report* 127 (August 2, 1999).

2. "Bogle on Brokers," *On Wall Street* (November 2000): 168.

3. John Bogle, *John Bogle on Investing: The First 50 Years* (New York: McGraw-Hill, 2001).

4. "Quantitative Analysis of Investor Behavior," www.dalbarinc.com, 2001.

5. William Bernstein, *The Intelligent Asset Allocator* (New York: McGraw Hill, 2001).

6. Transcript from *20/20* episode, November 27, 1992.

7. Zvi Bodie, Alex Kane, Alan J. Marcus, *Investments* (New York: McGraw Hill-College Div., 2001).

8. William Sharpe, "The Parable of the Money Managers," *The Financial Analysts' Journal* 32 (July/August 1976).

CHAPTER 9—THE PROTECTED INVESTOR: SMARTER, SAFER WAYS TO INVEST

1. Fischer Black and Myron Scholes, "The Pricing of Options and Corporate Liabilities," *Journal of Political Economy,* no. 81 (1973): 637–659.

2. Robert Cringely, "Fast Money," *Forbes ASAP* (April 11, 1994): 74.

3. Steve Cocheo, "Market-Linked CDs: Hope—or Hype—for the Deposit Starved?" *ABA Banking Journal* 93 (May 2001): 16.

4. "Investment Strategies for Personal Retirement," Federal Document Clearing House, congressional testimony, June 15, 1999.

5. Andrew Wahl, "What's Yours Is Mine," *Canadian Business* 73 (September 4, 2000): 9.

6. Lauren Bielski, "High Net Worth Investors Make New Choices," *ABA Banking Journal* 93 (August 2001): 7.

7. Paul J. Lim, "Hybrid Investments Offer Security—But at Some Cost," *U.S. News & World Report* 131 (July 2, 2001): 54.

8. Pat Regnier, "Is This Kind of Insurance Worth the Cost?" *Money* 27 (May 1998): 32.

9. Jean Sherman Chatzky, "A Walk on the Safe Side . . . Securities with Downside Protection Are Looking Good These Days," *Money* 30 (August 2001): 144.

10. "Annuity Sales: Using a Layered Approach," *National Underwriter* (August 7, 2000).

11. "Insurance Companies Offer Equity Index Annuities," *San Diego Business Journal* (November 29, 1999): 24.

12. "Reaching for the Man on the Street," *Euromoney* (November 2000).

CHAPTER 10—INVESTING FOR RETIREMENT

1. Thornton Parker, *What If Boomers Can't Retire?* (San Francisco: Berrett-Koehler, 2000), 15.

2. "Possible Pension Crisis Sparks Calls for Overhaul," *Congressional Quarterly* (August 9, 1997).

3. Edward N. Wolff, *Retirement Insecurity* (Washington D.C.: Economic Policy Institute, 2002), 27.

4. "Saving the Retirement We Earned," *Bloomberg Personal Finance* (November 2002).

5. Jane Bryant Quinn, "Burned! Why We Need to Fix the 401-K," *Newsweek* (August 19, 2002).

6. "Legal & Fiduciary Issues in Participant Directed 401-K Plans," *CPA Journal* (November 1999).

7. Quinn, "Burned!"

CHAPTER 11—REFORMING THE SYSTEM

1. Jack L. VanDerhei, "Company Stock in 401(K) Plans: Results of a Survey of ISCEBS Members," Employee Benefit Research Institute (January 31, 2002).

2. Jonathan Weisman, "Phony Prices May Hide Import-Export Profits from IRS," *Washington Post,* 1 November 2002.

3. Michael Maiello, "Tower of Babel," *Forbes* 170 (July 22, 2002).

4. "What Good Are Disclosures That Go Unread?" *Business Week,* March 26, 2002.

5. "NY Prosecutor Spitzer Attacks Merrill Lynch Research Unit," *Euroweek* (April 12, 2002).

6. "We Were Chumps to Rely on That 401K," *Medford Mail Tribune,* 15 August 2002.

7. Emanuel Hertz, *Abraham Lincoln: A New Portrait* (New York: Horace Liveright, 1931), 954.

APPENDIX A—USING OPTIONS TO REDUCE RISK

1. "Derivatives Revisited," *Journal of Accountancy* (May 2000): 35.

APPENDIX B CREDIT RATINGS

1. "About Our Ratings," A. M. Best Company, www.ambest.com.

Glossary

accumulation phase The period when an annuity owner can add money and accumulate assets tax deferred.

alpha A measure of risk relating to the specific security, rather than the overall market.

analyst An employee of a financial institution who makes buy and sell recommendations for specific companies after studying their business and financial data.

annual reset Also known as *annual ratchet*. An annuity design whereby the policyholder receives the greater of the appreciation in the equity index during a series of one-year periods at each policy anniversary date or the guaranteed fixed rate of return for the policy period.

annuity A contract sold by an insurance company that grows tax deferred and is designed to provide a series of payments to the holder, usually after retirement.

asset allocation The process of determining how to divide investments among different kinds of assets, such as stocks, bonds, real estate, and cash in an attempt to minimize risk.

balance sheet A summary of a company's assets, liabilities, and net worth at a specific point in time.

beta A tool for measuring the volatility of a given stock, mutual fund, or portfolio as compared to the overall market.

blue chip Stock of a large, national company with a solid record of stable earnings and/or dividend growth.

book value A company's common stock equity, equal to total assets minus liabilities, preferred stock, and intangible assets such as goodwill, as reported on its balance sheet.

call option (long) A contract that gives the holder the right to buy a certain quantity of a security at a specified price for a specified time.

call option (short)   A contract that gives the seller (writer) the obligation to sell a certain quantity of a security at a specified price for a specified time.

cap   The maximum interest that can be credited to a market-linked investment over a specified period of time.

Chartered Financial Analyst (CFA)   An individual who has passed tests in economics, accounting, security analysis, and money management, administered by the Institute of Chartered Financial Analysts.

Chartered Financial Consultant (ChFC)   An individual who has completed a program of economics, taxes, insurance, and investing.

Chartered Life Underwriter (CLU)   An individual who has completed training in life insurance and personal insurance planning.

Collateralized Mortgage Obligation (CMO)   A mortgage-backed, investment-grade bond that separates mortgage pools into different maturity classes, called *tranches*.

common stock   Securities representing ownership in a corporation, which entitle the holder to participate in the company's success through dividends and/or growth.

daily averaging   A method of determining the index level in an annuity to compare to the beginning level at reset. The closing index of each day is added together and divided by the number of days in the period.

dilution   The reduction in earnings per share or book value per share that occurs if all outstanding warrants and stock options are exercised and all convertible securities are converted.

diversification   A portfolio strategy designed to reduce risk by combining different categories of investments, such as stocks, bonds, and real estate and different investments within each category.

Dow Jones Industrial Average (Dow)   A price-weighted average of thirty actively traded blue-chip stocks, which is the most widely used indicator of the overall condition of the stock market.

earnings before interest, taxes, depreciation, and amortization (EBITDA)   An approximate measure of a company's operating cash flow based on earnings before the deduction of interest expenses, taxes, depreciation, and amortization.

earnings per share (EPS) Total earnings of a company divided by its total number of shares outstanding.

EBITDA See earnings before interest, taxes, depreciation, and amortization.

equity-index annuity A unique class of annuities that uses equity indexes as the basis for calculating the interest that will be credited to the policy. These are considered fixed annuities and include minimum guarantees with the potential for additional interest from the performance of stock market indexes without downside risk.

equity-linked note A debt instrument whose return on investment is tied to the equity markets, usually a stock index. These securities include minimum guarantees with the potential for additional interest from the performance of stock market indexes without downside risk.

Federal Deposit Insurance Corporation (FDIC) A federal agency that insures deposits in member banks and thrifts up to $100,000.

Federal Home Loan Mortgage Corporation (FHLMC or Freddie Mac) Government-chartered corporation, which offers mortgage-backed securities to investors. Principal and interest are guaranteed by FHLMC.

Federal National Mortgage Association (FNMA or Fannie Mae) A congressionally chartered corporation, which offers mortgage-backed securities to investors. Principal and interest payments are guaranteed by FNMA.

fee-based financial planning Financial planning services that are paid for on a flat fee or an hourly basis, rather than on a commission basis, in an attempt to minimize potential conflicts of interest.

fiduciary A person to whom property and/or power is entrusted for the benefit of another, often with the legal authority and duty to make decisions regarding financial matters.

financial planner An investment professional who helps individuals set and achieve their long-term financial goals, through investments, tax planning, asset allocation, risk management, retirement planning, and estate planning.

fixed annuity   An investment vehicle offered by insurance companies that guarantees a stream of fixed payments. The insurer assumes the investment risk.

Generally Accepted Accounting Principles (GAAP)   A widely accepted set of rules, conventions, standards, and procedures established by the Financial Accounting Standards Board for reporting a company's financial information.

goodwill   In a merger, goodwill is the amount by which the purchase price exceeds the net tangible assets of the acquired company.

Government National Mortgage Association (GNMA or Ginnie Mae)   A government-owned agency that offers mortgage-backed securities to investors. Guaranteed by the full faith and credit of the U.S. government.

index   A statistical indicator providing a representation of the value of its underlying securities.

indexing   An investment strategy that mitigates the risk of not performing as well as the market by designing a portfolio to mirror the performance of a stock index, such as the S&P 500.

inflation risk   The possibility that the shrinking purchasing power of a currency will reduce the value of assets or income.

initial public offering (IPO)   The first sale of stock by a company to the public.

invest   To put money to use in order to obtain profitable returns.

investment bank   A financial institution that acts as an underwriter for corporations issuing securities, but does not accept deposits or make loans.

liquidity   The ability to quickly convert an asset into cash without a reduction in the price.

market capitalization   The value of a company according to the market, calculated by multiplying the number of outstanding shares by the price per share.

money manager   An individual who is responsible for the entire financial portfolio of an individual or other entity. A money manager receives payment in exchange for choosing and monitoring appropriate investments for the client.

mortgage-backed security (MBS)   Security backed by mortgages, such as those issued by Ginnie Mae, Fannie Mae, or Freddie Mac.

point-to-point   An annuity design whereby the policyholder receives the higher of the appreciation of an equity index over a specified period (for example, five or eight years starting on policy issue date) or a guaranteed fixed rate of return.

pooling of interests   One method of accounting for a company merger, in which the balance sheet items of the two companies are added together.

preferred stock   Capital stock that provides a definite dividend, which takes precedence over common stock dividends.

preservation of capital   An investment strategy that has as its priority avoiding the risk of loss.

price-to-earnings (P/E) ratio   A tool for comparing companies' market valuation. It is determined by dividing the current market price of the stock by its reported earnings per share over the previous twelve months.

pro forma   Hypothetical financial statements that have one or more assumptions built into the data.

put option (long)   A contract that gives the holder the right to sell a certain quantity of a security at a specified price for a specified period of time.

put option (short)   A contract that gives the seller the obligation to buy a certain quantity of a security at a specified price for a specified time.

risk   The quantifiable probability of loss or less-than-expected returns.

risk averse   The desire to avoid risk unless adequately compensated for it; the attitude of most investors.

risk management   The process of determining how to best handle exposure to risk.

Securities Investor Protection Corporation (SIPC)   A nonprofit membership corporation established by Congress that insures securities and cash in customer accounts up to $500,000 (up to $100,000 on cash) in the event of brokerage bankruptcy.

shareholder   An individual or entity that owns shares of stock (stockholder) in a corporation or mutual fund.

stock   A financial instrument that establishes an ownership position in a corporation.

stock option   A contract on a specific stock giving the holder the right but not the obligation to buy or sell the stock at a predetermined price by a specific date.

variable annuity   An investment vehicle offered by insurance companies that provides future payments based on the performance of the securities selected. The insured takes on the investment risk.

INDEX

Italic page numbers refer to entries in tables, illustrations, or chapter opening quotes.

ABOUT THE AUTHOR

 EDWARD J. WINSLOW JR. is the senior partner and founder of PM Investments and is one of the most creative and knowledgeable financial consultants in the country. He avoids traditional investments such as stocks and mutual funds while providing a unique strategy for building and safeguarding wealth.

Ed was the founder as well as chairman of First Affirmative Financial Network, the nation's first broker/dealer to specialize in socially responsible investing. He was also founder and president of First American Financial Cooperative, the nation's first cooperatively owned financial planning firm.

Ed has been recognized in *Who's Who in the West* and *Who's Who in Finance and Industry.* He was the first recipient of the prestigious SRI Service Award recognizing his unique contribution to the social investment industry.

Before going into the investment field in the early 1980s, Ed served as treasurer of a credit union, accounting supervisor for a major computer manufacturer, accounting/financial officer of a property and casualty insurance company, and as an accountant for a major airline.

Ed has achieved numerous professional designations: Certified Public Accountant (CPA), Certified Financial Planner (CFP), Chartered Financial Consultant (ChFC), Chartered Life Underwriter (CLU), Fellow Life Management Institute (FLMI), and Associate in Risk Management (ARM).

Contact Ed at Protect Money Investments, P.O. Box 66, Jacksonville, OR 97530; web site: www.protectmoney.com; email: ed@protectmoney.com.

Berrett-Koehler Publishers

B errett-Koehler is an independent publisher of books and other publications at the leading edge of new thinking and innovative practice on work, business, management, leadership, stewardship, career development, human resources, entrepreneurship, and global sustainability.

Since the company's founding in 1992, we have been committed to creating a world that works for all by publishing books that help us to integrate our values with our work and work lives, and to create more humane and effective organizations.

We have chosen to focus on the areas of work, business, and organizations, because these are central elements in many people's lives today. Furthermore, the work world is going through tumultuous changes, from the decline of job security to the rise of new structures for organizing people and work. We believe that change is needed at all levels—individual, organizational, community, and global—and our publications address each of these levels.

To find out about our new books,
special offers,
free excerpts,
and much more,
subscribe to our free monthly eNewsletter at

www.bkconnection.com

Please see next pages for other books
from Berrett-Koehler Publishers

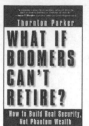

Berrett-Koehler books and audios
are available at quantity discounts
for orders of 10 or more copies.

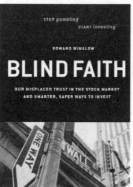

Blind Faith

Our Misplaced Trust in the Stock Market—and Smarter, Safer Ways to Invest

Edward Winslow

Paperback original
250 pages
ISBN 1-57675-252-6
Item #52526-415 $14.95

To find out about discounts on orders of 10 or more
copies for individuals, corporations, institutions, and
organizations, please call us toll-free at (800) 929-2929.

To find out about our discount programs for resellers,
please contact our Special Sales department at (415)
288-0260; Fax: (415) 362-2512. Or email us at
bkpub@bkpub.com.

Subscribe to our free e-newsletter!

To find out about what's happening at Berrett-Koehler
and to receive announcements of our new books,
special offers, free excerpts, and much more,
subscribe to our free monthly e-newsletter at
www.bkconnection.com.

Berrett-Koehler Publishers
PO Box 565, Williston, VT 05495-9900
Call toll-free! **800-929-2929** 7 am-9 pm Eastern Standard Time
Or fax your order to 802-864-7627
For fastest service order online: **www.bkconnection.com**